Acknowledgement

My thanks and my appreciation go to the following people: Vi Freeland for the paintings she created for the cover and also the bear holding the balloons with Mary Kay's note; Shelee Bush for the cover design; Joyce Curtis, my assistant for her work in helping me assemble the book; Kristin Maurice, and Judi Jordan for proof reading.

Contents

Acknowledgement   vii

Preface   xi

1   A Most Unlikely Friendship   1

2   Could It Be a Con?   7

3   Guilty of Stinkin' Thinkin'   11

4   A Female Brain Is Worth More than Fifty Cents
on the Dollar   17

5   The Look of a Golden Rule Company   25

6   The Heart of a Leader When Her People Face Violence   41

7   Dear God, Where Are You?   49

8   Life Skills Learned from Mary Kay   53

9   We Were Not Created to Be Lone Rangers   63

10   The Dawn Will Come   69

11   Through the Valley of the Shadow   73

12   One More Parallel before the Curtain Begins to Fall   89

13   A Victorious Finish for the Most Important
American Woman of the Twentieth Century   93

Postscript   99

Appendix   105

Preface

This book is a very personal look at Mary Kay Ash, founder of Mary Kay Cosmetics. *The Heart of a Leader* explores Mary Kay's legacy and her four magnificent passions. All four have played a prominent role in my own life.

Her first passion was to provide an opportunity for women to improve their economic situation. This grand obsession was the driving force in founding Mary Kay Cosmetics. The effects of this great work are evident everywhere and continue today.

Her second passion was to instill in women a confidence in their God-given abilities. This was closely associated with her first passion, for it soon became evident that for women to be able to advance financially, each woman had to have some bit of faith that this might be possible for *her*. Mary Kay realized that many women were crippled in this area of their thinking, so she set about to teach women to believe in their abilities and to learn to dream big dreams. The results of this tremendous endeavor will continue for generations. Also, I believe Mary Kay would want me to emphasize what she believed was the key to all of her successes: she publicly credited all of her success to the fact that she took God for her senior partner, the controlling partner.

During the early years, it was necessary for Mary Kay to focus on these two objectives in order to successfully launch Mary Kay Cosmetics. Her third great cause was to work toward eradicating breast cancer. During the sixties, breasts were never mentioned from a public platform. Thus a woman's experience of the terrible disease of breast cancer was likely to be a terrifying, largely private experience that she faced virtually alone. A diagnosis was widely considered a death sentence, in part because in many cases the cancer was discovered too late. Women were quite literally scared to death. Society behaved like an ostrich with its head stuck in the sand. Women acted as if the menace was not real, at least not until they heard the words "breast cancer." The ravages of the disease that was attacking her "daughters" (as Mary Kay often referred to the consultants and directors of her company) outraged Mary Kay and brought out the champion in her. She began to campaign for information, education, and funding for cancer research. She dared to talk about breast cancer from the stage at the annual seminar. Due to the fact that she was already so revered and loved among women, it is my belief that she did more than any other public figure to advance this cause, perhaps even more than the courageous First Lady Betty Ford. One of the fruits of her labors was the formation of the Mary Kay Ash Charitable Foundation (www. mkacf.org).

Mary Kay took action because she realized that having a positive attitude meant not living in a "pink bubble" or feeling like we will not be affected as long as we do nothing. Mary Kay faced cancer's evil and set out to find the magic bullet. She went about empowering women, teaching us to courageously face cancer and to make a difference. Although there is still a long way to go and the magic bullet has yet to be found, tremendous strides have been made. While Mary Kay was not the first or only courageous pioneer to attack the problem, she was instrumental in making great advancements possible. Because of her, breast cancer will never wield the power over women's lives that it once did.

The foundation is also directed towards her fourth passion, which was ending violence against women and children. This passion emerged as her work expanded and her awareness of this sinister problem facing women grew. Like an iceberg, largely hidden from view, one only caught glimpses of the violence being perpetrated against women and children. As with breast cancer, this was a subject that had no general public acknowledgement. Prior to the opening of the first women's shelter in the early seventies, there was no place for a woman to go to escape abuse. Women were trapped in a cycle of violence. This situation was not acceptable, and Mary Kay wanted to do more than just cover up the scars of abused women with makeup. Consequently, she determined to break the silence of another public taboo.

The Mary Kay Foundation is doing excellent work to help battered women by educating the public and funding shelters for women. However, in spite of the efforts of the Mary Kay Foundation and scores of other heroic groups, our national will to address the problem of violence is still in its infancy. It seems to be in a spot similar to where breast cancer was in the seventies. This branch of the excellent Mary Kay Foundation is relatively unknown, and even those who know it often regard it simply as something to give a bit of money to here and there rather than a place for personal involvement. This is not surprising, since I have found that most people do not want to talk or even think about violence. Unfortunately, even among Mary Kay directors and consultants, I found that not one single person with whom I talked, other than those directors who had actually done fundraisers for the foundation, had ever visited the portion of the Mary Kay Web site that is dedicated to breaking the silence on domestic violence. When a widespread passion to make a difference ignites and people realize that it could happen to them, the foundation will become more than a place to give a little money occasionally.

Progress is difficult to achieve as long as people say to themselves, "It's not my problem. It won't happen to my family or me. It only happens to other people in crime-infested areas or in the lowest economic stratum." On the contrary, the fact is that domestic violence occurs in all strata of society. The grim statistic is this: one out of four women will be the victim of violence in her lifetime. Can you imagine the problems a woman encounters if she is being abused by a husband who is a respected professional, maybe a lawyer, a doctor, a judge, or a minister? Where can she go? Today, violence is on the rise and increasing to a point Mary Kay could hardly imagine.

Many of our churches are not addressing the subject of rape and murder either. One secular bookstore regularly sold five or more copies a week of my book *Lethal Friendship*, the account of my fight to keep a serial killer behind bars, but a Christian bookstore in the same area did not sell a single copy. When I related this story to a friend of mine from church, she said, "Sue, I certainly understand, because when I go to a Christian bookstore, I don't want to be depressed. I am looking for inspiration." This is the same kind of response that the mention of breast cancer elicited in the past. However, as we discovered with education about breast cancer, knowledge about ways to prevent violence can be very empowering and positive.

I think that Mary Kay would be proud of us for carrying on her legacy. If she could speak to us today, would she again ask us to passionately look for that magic bullet and this time direct it against violence? I think she would. I know from experience that Mary Kay people, when motivated, can be a force to be reckoned with in their communities. In the past, Mary Kay set the standard, and now, with this next generation, let us grasp that mantle of leadership and do it again.

The *Heart of a Leader* is my tribute to Mary Kay and the profound influence she had on my life. To show Mary Kay's heart for women, I have chosen to use stories about her impact on one woman's life, my own, even though I am just one of the hundreds of thousands of women impacted by her. I have written about events that I know and experienced. It is my hope that these stories help capture some of the essence of Mary Kay.

The opinions expressed are mine and are not meant to represent the opinions of any group or organization.

To my beloved
friend — Sue
Hang in there!
Love,
Mary Kay

1
A Most Unlikely Friendship

Mary Kay Ash and I first met in her rented office space on Majesty Drive in Dallas, Texas, before the first Mary Kay building was built. What I saw was a very attractive woman who was perfectly groomed, with flawless makeup and every hair in place. This was in 1967, when most of the country was following the no-makeup, flower-child image. Mary Kay, on the other hand, reflected the fashionable look of women in large southern cities, who wore a full array of color cosmetics.

She moved with amazing grace on the very highest of high heels. Compared to my five feet, seven inch frame, she was considerably shorter, even in those spike heels. Even so, I didn't think of her as being small in stature; she was so poised and confident that she seemed to meet my gaze at eye level. Her presence was so engaging that it was impossible to think of her as a small woman.

She was gracious and welcoming when I was introduced to her. She was the kind of person who drew you in with her warmth. I wish I had paid more attention to every detail of that first conversation, because at the time I didn't realize that I had just met a woman on a mission! With her enormous empathy for women in trouble, Mary Kay was determined to enrich women's lives. I had no idea what a tremendous impact she would have on my own life and how she would change it forever.

Her sense of mission started early in life. Beginning at the tender age of seven, Mary Kay shouldered great responsibility in her family. Because her father was ill, her mother had to work long hours to earn the family income. Consequently, by necessity, Mary Kay had the task of cooking for her father. Mary Kay must have had a remarkable mother. Since she lacked the freedom to be there in person for her daughter, she turned to the telephone, and talking to her daughter from work became the way they communicated.

In the process of performing essential tasks, her mother constantly said, "You can do it." Mary Kay thus learned early in life that she could overcome adverse situations. At an age where most children were cautiously holding the hand of an adult to cross the street, Mary Kay was learning to use the city bus to do shopping in downtown Houston, a task normally reserved for adults. In the process, she acquired a can-do attitude, establishing the pattern of an achiever. Later, when she founded her company, it was natural for her to approach the task with a positive attitude. High expectations and a consistently positive attitude became the hallmarks of her life. These attributes were coupled with her faith, which taught her to put God first and to focus on the needs of others. From her mother she also learned the power of the encouraging word. Mary Kay's life growing up was too busy for her to become either lonely or self-absorbed.

The circumstances of my childhood produced a very different upbringing. Both of us were greatly loved by our parents, but my parents had both the means and the willingness to protect and indulge me. Due to their experiences of hard work associated with growing up on a farm and the hardships of living through the Great Depression in their young adult years, my parents were determined that my life would be better. In addition, my parents married late in life and were told that my mother could not have children, and this probably increased their desire to protect me. We were not rich, but any extravagance was directed toward me. I was not even required to perform chores. Growing up I faced no challenges. I loved my parents and knew that I was loved and well cared for, yet I grew up lonely, self-conscious, and sad.

It was against all odds that I would ever even meet this positive, dynamic woman, let alone become her friend. In 1963, when Mary

Kay founded the company in Dallas, my husband and I were living on the other side of the world in Lahore, Pakistan, where we served as Methodist missionaries for five years. My husband was an architect and engineer assigned by the mission board to build the United Christian Hospital complex. Upon our return to the States in 1965, we could have found a job in any state or returned to Austin, Texas, where we had lived before going overseas. Neither of us had ever lived in Dallas, but my husband's first job offer was in Dallas. Later, after our move to Dallas, he was offered a job in Michigan through an engineer we had met while in Pakistan. If the Michigan offer had come first and we had located in Michigan rather than Dallas, it is extremely unlikely that Mary Kay and I would have become friends, because once I relocated to Michigan, I never returned to Texas to live.

In those years, Mary Kay Cosmetics was strictly word of mouth. There was no advertising or marketing campaign. Even if there had been, I certainly never would have guessed that I would come to know the founder in a special way.

There were even more daunting obstacles to my becoming involved with Mary Kay. I was not remotely interested in cosmetics, which of course had become a primary focus for Mary Kay. I did not host home parties, nor did I attend them! I wanted *nothing* to do with sales. That, to me, was a dirty word. Combine sales with cosmetics and you have something I could not, in my wildest imagination, have pictured myself doing. I had a master's degree and a career as a teacher. To make matters worse I was an introvert. Now add skepticism and a negative attitude. I didn't even *want* a positive attitude. At that time I associated positive thinking with voodoo or magic rather than reality. And I certainly placed a high value on reality! Considering the fact that *sales* was a dirty word to me, it amazes me that I would find myself standing in Mary Kay's office being introduced to her and then have her become my friend. I definitely did not fit the image of what I thought it would take to be successful in cosmetics. In my view, the consultant would need to be ultra-young, ultra-beautiful, and ultra-blonde. I was none of the above.

A few months after we moved to Dallas, my former college roommate, Mary Jane, who was also living in Dallas, invited me

3

to a luncheon she was having for her niece. The luncheon was a kind of bribe to get a group of women together so that her niece could demonstrate a skin care line from this new little local cosmetic company called *Beauty by Mary Kay*. Since Mary Jane ordinarily did not do this type of thing, only family and close friends were invited. I decided to attend the luncheon, but I had no intention of buying anything, so I went with an empty purse.

During the course of trying the skin care treatment on my face, the niece mentioned that the deep cleansing, which was a result of this five-step basic skin care regime, helped to clear blemish-prone skin. That caught my attention, because I joked that I was the oldest adolescent around. Trips to the dermatologist hadn't cleared my face. At the price of $15.95, I figured, "What do I have to lose? It's about the price of one trip to the doctor's office without the additional cost of medication." I went back home and got the money to purchase the set. Even so, I really didn't expect much.

Amazingly, nine months later my skin was clear and I needed to reorder. My pastor and his wife were friends, and he had noticed that I no longer had skin eruptions on my face. His wife, Martha, decided the cosmetics must be pretty good, so she scheduled a class and I attended. Martha's consultant, Doris, was closer to my age. She was also a schoolteacher and not a total beauty. This lady talked more about the founder and the company. She painted an extraordinary picture of both Mary Kay and her company. In spite of my attitude, there was something intangible about the opportunity that drew me to this business. It was like a Cinderella story. Women like me were making more per month than I could ever imagine. Because my faith and family were important to me, I liked Mary Kay's idea about putting "God first, family second, and career third." It sounded attractive to work for a company that applied the principle of faith and conducted all their business by treating every person with respect, treating them the way you would want to be treated.

Doris spoke about getting in on a ground floor business opportunity. That sounded exciting. In addition to earning good money by conducting skin care classes, she talked of women who had become directors and were earning an additional director's bonus of two thousand dollars *a month!* The mention of the director's commission really got my attention! Two thousand dollars was almost half of an entire year's salary for me. In 1967, as a teacher with a master's degree and five years of experience, I was not even making five thousand a year in the Dallas public schools.

The company began to sound very interesting to me for several reasons. As a teacher, I didn't like the situation of not being able to help out at my daughters' schools with their field trips. In addition, I wanted to be there when they came home from school. One of my biggest reasons, however, was that I could see the handwriting on the wall with my marriage. I felt at some point I would be raising my daughters by myself. I didn't want a career that would not allow me to be at home with my daughters.

A small crack had opened up in my mind. It was open just enough to start me on a pathway that would lead to an exciting adventure that has now spanned forty years. But I'm getting ahead of myself. Before I started on my journey, I had to uncover the answer to this burning question: "Was it legit?"

2
Could It Be a Con?

Although the Mary Kay business sounded great, before I could really move forward, I needed to find my own answer to that nagging question, "Could it be some sort of a con?" Money was the primary motivating factor in my beginning days with this business. However, although money was important to me, the way I made money was even more important. I wondered, "Could a company actually operate under the principle of 'Do unto others as you would have them do unto you'? Or could all this talk about faith be just a slogan … just a pious statement for public consumption? What would a company that actually practiced its faith in a business setting and practiced 'treating others as you would have them treat you' look like in the day-to-day world of business?" Since I was skeptical about everything, including Mary Kay herself, I spent the first few months trying to decide, "Is she for real?"

Since Mary Kay Cosmetics was not yet four years old and I lived right there in Dallas, I could observe the company up close and personal. What I discovered led me to become involved with Mary Kay Inc. I have stayed in the company for forty years because I was attracted not only to Mary Kay's leadership style but also to her integrity. I watched as she turned down operations to advance the company's interest because she questioned the ethics involved. When a lawyer told her, "But Mary Kay, it's legal," her answer came swiftly and definitively: "Yes, but it's not right, and we aren't going to do it!" And she didn't! She was genuine, I discovered. The practice of the Golden Rule was very much a part of her very being. Mary Kay believed in providing real value for her customer's money. Mary Kay herself was frugal with her own money, so she believed she should respect her customer's money as well.

As I became sold on her and the company, I still had no idea I would have the extraordinary privilege of having Mary Kay as my friend. Neither did I know how much I would grow through my association with her, for I brought all my firmly entrenched negative attitudes with me into my new venture. With all of my negativity, I could have been a real pain to be around during those early days. Fortunately, I was shy, so I did not express my feelings aloud to anyone. My Mary Kay friends never knew how bad my attitude was in the beginning.

From the start I did do one thing right. I attended everything: the weekly sales meetings, workshops, guest events, and the annual seminar. It was here that I continued learning about the company. The meetings were fun and inspiring. We shared ideas and were given new ones. We learned from our mistakes without ever feeling put down. I always came away from the meetings motivated and feeling good about myself. Before joining Mary Kay, I had a rather serious nature, so I had to learn to put fun in my life. I also made new friends at these events and began learning life skills that related not only to my business but also to my life outside of Mary Kay. I began to see growth in myself, and I enjoyed the changes taking place in my attitude.

Since I was gaining more and more respect for this business, I began to realize that part of my skepticism was not directed toward Mary Kay Cosmetics itself but rather toward sales in general. Although I was starting to be satisfied that Mary Kay was indeed trustworthy, the distrust I had for the whole field of sales lingered. Part of my sales training was learning about the psychology of personal growth. This was helpful. In order to be successful in sales, it is useful to understand other people's points of view. Obviously, we don't want to bore a person who just wants to hear the highpoints by giving them the same amount of information that an analytical person would need in order to feel comfortable. As I began to understand a bit about psychology, my stereotyped idea of salespeople began to change. A keynote speaker at one of my first seminars finally convinced me that it is just as honorable to sell as it is to buy.

Coinciding with the life skills I was learning in Mary Kay was a course I was attending at my church about how to relate to different personality styles. My best friend and next-door neighbor, Betty Collins, and I went together. By answering a series of questions, we learned to identify four basic personality styles: the energetic "take charge" kind of personality, who likes information short and to the point; the energetic, outgoing, "social magnet" personality, who wants all the fun details; the slower-paced, social, agreeable style; and the analytic, detail-oriented style. This enhanced what I was beginning to learn in Mary Kay through the teaching of Bill Cantrell. I was both shocked and fascinated by the very different thought processes in which individuals engage given the same set of circumstances. I came to see a concrete example of this in my relationship with my friend Betty. I was shocked when I grasped the idea that I was driving Betty a bit crazy by the way I interacted with her in ordinary, mundane situations. A case in point was when I popped in for a visit with Betty. She routinely inquired what I would like to drink, offering ice tea, lemonade, various kinds of pop, and so forth; and I habitually responded, "It really doesn't matter." We could literally spend five to ten minutes discussing what I wanted to drink. In my mind, I wanted to cause her no trouble, and I had this weird sense that this was somehow being polite. This was not the message she was receiving. Looking back, I see how strangely my insecurities were manifested. Through the study of personality styles, I acquired skills that have added depth to friendships, increased joy in life, and also smoothed out rough spots in dealing with customers. Steadily I began to understand, through the seminars, workshops, and sales meetings, how our thoughts affect our lives and how our quality of life is enhanced or diminished by our choice of attitude.

Although I was changing, this did not mean that my business was thriving. Of course, my problem could have had something to do with the fact that I absolutely refused to do some of the things that were suggested. I wasn't obnoxious. I didn't argue. I just didn't do it.

This was particularly true in regard to the words Mary Kay gave us to use. "That doesn't sound like me," I thought. I failed to recognize that it was a new field to me and that Mary Kay was the expert. I was afraid of sounding phony if I used someone else's words. So I stumbled around using my own words. The results were less than exciting.

Although I was still new in my career, I had discovered that Mary Kay was genuine. I also recognized that what I was doing in the business wasn't working, while others around me were having success. Since I realized my career could use a boost, I was open to attending the annual seminar. And I was ready to hear words and ideas that not only enriched my life but also, I am convinced, contributed greatly to saving my life on two occasions. I was ready to meet the man who would provide those.

3
Guilty of Stinkin' Thinkin'

At the annual Mary Kay Seminar, an awesome man with an odd name energized the stage. Because of this new venture, I was seated in the audience. This put me in a position to be powerfully influenced by the man with the strange name and, from my perspective, an even stranger idea about how to achieve success. Our keynote speaker was Zig Ziglar. He captivated us with his words, enthusiasm, motivational stories, and fun demonstrations of the truths he was teaching. Ordinarily, a person's memory of a speech is virtually gone by the end of a week or two. But Zig was so memorable that I remember much of what he said; those words are still enriching my life over thirty years later. In his speech he nailed me, for I realized I was guilty of what he called stinkin' thinkin'.

As I listened, he threw out a challenge. He promised that if we accepted his challenge, it would change our lives for the better. In fact, Zig guaranteed a positive change. He asked for our decision before he would tell us what was involved. His proposition went something like this: "It won't cost you any money, it will take no extra time, it won't hurt anyone, it's legal … but … it may make you feel a 'lit-tle bit' foolish. Will you agree?" I agreed.

The next day was a Sunday, and my family awakened to some bizarre behavior on my part. As I sleepily rolled out of bed, I clapped my hands together and loudly announced, as instructed, "Oh boy! It's going to be a great day!" Then, according to Zig's script, I marched downstairs singing at the top of my lungs! Volume was important, Zig had said, because singing timidly makes it possible to go right on worrying and thinking negative thoughts. We were told to select a positive song and sing it heartily for at least fifteen minutes. I chose "The Impossible Dream." By the time my family came downstairs, I had their full attention! Their ordinarily serious mom was acting a bit crazy, but it was a fun kind of crazy. Following the program that Zig had prescribed, I proclaimed, "Guess what we are having for breakfast today?" On Sundays I routinely fixed waffles for breakfast, but as my daughters and my husband looked at me warily, I declared, "We are having waffles!" With that, the giggles turned into laughter. I found myself enjoying my family's reaction and being able, for the first time, to enjoy not taking myself so seriously. I found myself taking pleasure in laughing at my own strange behavior. That Sunday was the first time arguments did not flare and we actually arrived at church with all four of us in a good mood. It felt great.

The program to which I had committed myself required that I keep up this same activity for twenty-one days. I had made a promise, so each day I continued to clap my hands and proclaim, "Today is going to be a great day!" and then launch into fifteen minutes of singing. Slowly the routine began to make a difference each day. And by this time in my life, I wanted things to change. A sense of joy had been lacking in my life. Life was flat, dull, and fearful. I was frequently obsessing about remote possibilities. For example, my daughter received a minor scratch from a stray cat, and I lay awake at night shaking with fear that the cat was rabid and that my daughter would contract rabies. My family thought I was losing my mind when I said I wanted to contact radio stations to help us look for a nondescript stray cat. Time passed and the scratch healed, but not the pervasive feelings of a looming evil.

Although it was never diagnosed medically, it seems likely to me now that I had been living with depression for a period of years. Each day I awakened with a sense of dread, a feeling of impending doom. These ominous feelings arose before anything really bad had ever happened to me. They had peaked during graduate school, disappeared when I graduated and went to work, and then reappeared after I was married.

If I was doing anything special or traveling that day, the feelings intensified. I felt like a cartoon character that had this black cloud over her head. Wherever I moved, the cloud followed me and was always overhead. It wasn't a fulfilling way to live, so I was open to Zig's influence. I was eager to continue when I realized his program was working for me. When I started singing vigorously each morning, that black cloud did not lift immediately, but I noticed that sometime in the latter part of the morning the cloud was gone! I felt so different, so much lighter, without that dark mass that hung over me constantly. Without warning, however, the gloom would sometimes roll back in. When that happened, I would give myself an extra session and spend another fifteen minutes singing vigorously.

One day while I was driving to a skin care class, the gray cloud was again covering me, so I decided to sing. Since the windows of my car were rolled up, I figured it was safe. No one could hear me. I was on an off-ramp beside the freeway, stopped at a traffic light, and my singing was not producing any results. I needed a mood change fast, because I was nearing my hostess's home, so I began to accompany my singing by energetically pounding on the steering wheel in time to the music. As I was doing so, I happened to glance to my left at the truck that was sitting next to me at the traffic light. The driver was convulsed with laughter as he looked down at me. Our eyes met, and I too began to roar with laughter. I could only imagine what he must have thought about that crazy woman he had seen at the traffic stop. I am sure I made his day and provided him with a story he could tell for quite some time. He surely made my day, and the world was suddenly bright again.

Zig had convinced me that I was guilty of what he called "stinkin' thinkin'." The lessons that he taught from that seminar stage so many years ago have literally been a lifesaver to me during a couple of the most devastating periods of my life, ones that I will touch on in later chapters. I didn't burst out with loud cheery singing in the midst of those debilitating times, but I had learned that music bypasses the conscious mind and speaks directly to the spirit. Today I am more likely to be singing songs of faith. Singing reminds me to focus on almighty God instead of the problem. I learned that it is impossible to focus on two things at the same time, therefore you can force your mind to shift from dwelling on unspeakable horror to thinking about things that are good and true, such as a small flower or a neighbor's act of kindness. I am so glad that God also has a sense of humor and that he found a way to remind me not to relapse into taking myself so seriously. He did it through Sunny, my daughter's Brittany spaniel. Sunny apparently does not appreciate my singing, because whenever I start to sing, he tucks his ears in and heads for the opposite side of the house.

Zig also helped dispel my negative feeling about sales as an occupation. He taught me that the word "sales" is derived from a Norwegian word that means "to serve." Mary Kay taught consultants and directors to do business with integrity and never sell someone anything that was not in that person's best interest. As a director, my job was not only to serve my customers but also my consultants.

In spite of what I learned from Zig, I still needed to learn to believe in the necessity of following Mary Kay's instructions. Finally, I decided to go ahead and act as if I believed her. I decided to try her ideas and use her words to close my classes and book future appointments. I would just have to wait and see what was going to happen. The first time I used Mary Kay's words was at the close of a class where a customer had just purchased a complete collection for herself and a men's skin care basic for her husband. I said to her, "At every class I always select a couple of people I would most like to have as my next hostess, and today I have selected you. Tell me, is there any reason you can't have a class?" I was shocked to hear her respond, "Yes, I'll have a class."

Mary Kay had also told me repeatedly to read Napoleon Hill's classic, *Think and Grow Rich*. But it was not until nine months after I started my career in Mary Kay that I decided to take her advice. When I did, there was almost an instant confirmation of her advice. On the very day that I sat down and started reading, I received a phone call from a total stranger. Hill's book had reinforced Mary Kay's teaching and given me the belief and confidence to talk to the stranger on the other end of the phone. The woman asked me about how to become a Mary Kay consultant. She became my very first business partner. That convinced me. I decided that I would make a practice of doing the things Mary Kay taught.

I was finally becoming teachable and, as a result, more successful. I planned on becoming a director in Dallas and living there for the rest of my life. Then my husband accepted a partnership offer from an engineering company in Michigan. At that time there were no directors in Michigan, Ohio, Indiana, or Illinois, which meant I would have no director within driving distance to help me. This was both an opportunity and, at the same time, a setback to my plans. In Dallas, I was on the threshold of sponsoring the number of consultants required to begin qualifying to become a director. Although I would not lose any on my team of consultants in the move, I would be required to recruit seven more from the mid-Michigan area where I would live. This was difficult for two reasons. First, I had not yet established credibility, because I knew only one person in the entire state; and second, I was moving to an area that had had a rash of failed pyramid-scheme home businesses, an area where garages and basements were filled with either water purifiers or cosmetics. People had been recruited into these businesses with the idea that they didn't have to sell anything: "Just sign up other people who want a business opportunity." These businesses that used a "get rich quick" approach had few customers; the products were often just transferred from one person's garage to the new owner's basement. The companies soon went out of business, leaving people stuck with hundreds, even thousands of dollars worth of product in their homes. I became acquainted with people who had ten to twenty thousand dollars worth of product. Mary Kay Cosmetics was not yet known in Michigan, so people were justifiably skeptical.

The positive side was that it did give me the opportunity to become Michigan's first director a little over eighteen months after I moved there. As a new director, I was on my own. This was long before the Internet and a time when long-distance phone service was expensive. Because I had no local help, I frequently wrote letters to Mary Kay asking for her advice. In retrospect, I realize that the move actually caused my friendship with Mary Kay to grow.

4   A Female Brain Is Worth More than Fifty Cents on the Dollar

When I was living in Dallas, I seldom took advantage of the fact that Mary Kay's office door was always open. I could have walked through her door for a visit every week after the sales meeting. After I moved away, I wished that I had popped in more often and sought her counsel. However, when I moved to Michigan and had no one to help me, I didn't hesitate to take up pen and paper. Even after the staff began to grow at Mary Kay corporate headquarters in Dallas, the thought never entered my brain to write anyone other than Mary Kay. When I had an idea I got excited about, I wrote directly to Mary Kay, and when I had a question, it never occurred to me to write anyone else on the staff. My letters were always welcomed and answered enthusiastically. In most cases, I received an answer by return mail. This continued throughout her lifetime. Not until after her first stroke did anyone else ever send me a letter in answer to one I had addressed to Mary Kay. Occasionally, I picked up the phone and called her.

In June 1971 I became Michigan's first director. In pioneering Mary Kay Cosmetics in Michigan, I faced, on a much smaller scale, several of the same types of challenges Mary Kay had faced when she opened the company in Dallas. Since Mary Kay Cosmetics was still unknown in Michigan, I needed to find a way to establish local credibility and acceptance, so we invested about three thousand dollars in publicity in the Lansing and Ann Arbor areas. Unfortunately, we did this before consulting with Mary Kay. When I shared with her what I had done and excitedly asked how many extra phone lines I should install in my office to prepare for the orders that would come pouring in as a result of the advertising, her answer was, "None!" Then Mary Kay shared her own costly debacle in the field of paid advertising. She told me, "We knew that placing ads on local TV was too expensive for our budget; so we decided to put a large ad in the local newspapers. In order to handle the huge volume of business we anticipated pouring in, we started planning such things as installing additional banks of phones and hiring and training new temporary workers to man the phones. Much to our dismay, we found that no additional phones or staff were needed to handle the less than a dozen unproductive calls that resulted."

This experience led her to conclude that the most effective advertising was person to person and woman to woman. It would be many years before the company decided to again pay for advertising. My own experience confirmed what Mary Kay told me. For that three thousand dollar investment, I made one sale, a skin freshener, which retailed for four dollars. After that, I no longer needed convincing that there is no shortcut to building a foundation based on customers who see results and receive excellent service.

During the first few years after I joined the company, Mary Kay and I began to share a variety of life circumstances. A couple of years after moving to Michigan, my apprehensions about my marriage came true and I became separated from my husband. As a consequence, my Mary Kay income became even more essential. Mary Kay's mentorship also became more important to me as I learned how to negotiate life as a single parent.

Until I heard of Mary Kay's experiences with discrimination against women, I had been in a state of denial that such a practice still existed during this enlightened period in our nation's history. I vividly remember how I burned with outrage when she told us the story of how a former sales company had treated her. A new young man had been hired and assigned to Mary Kay for her to train and mentor. In order to learn the ropes, the young man accompanied her for a year as her assistant. He watched and learned as she led the company in record growth that year. At year's end, Mary Kay had opened more than a couple of dozen new states for her company. But instead of reaping the rewards of a job well done, her trainee became her boss. It was *he*, rather than Mary Kay, who benefited from all the business that Mary Kay had developed!

When my husband and I moved to East Lansing, Michigan, we had leased a home. When we separated, my husband returned to Texas and the girls and I remained in the home for five months. Six weeks before the lease was to expire, I received a letter asking if we wanted to renew the lease. I responded immediately. I informed them that I wanted to renew the lease but explained that my husband had moved back to Texas. Yet in spite of the fact that I had paid the rent and paid it early each month for six months, I did not receive a lease to sign. After waiting for several weeks, I contacted them again and told them I had not received the papers to sign. At that point they lied and said I would be getting the lease in the mail. So I waited. The papers did not arrive. So I called and asked bluntly if they had failed to send them because my husband wasn't there. I knew that this was discrimination and that it was illegal, but to my surprise I was told yes. Perhaps they didn't know that I knew the law, or possibly they counted on the likelihood that I was too busy trying to work and take care of my family to challenge them. They were right. I was on emotional overload, so I didn't fight it. I had thought six months of rent paid on time would have proven I was a good renter.

Although I didn't have a lease, they didn't tell me to move, so I continued to pay the rent. After a couple of months, I began to feel easier, but I was still very careful to see that the rent arrived early. A year passed, and I began to think that renting by the month wasn't so bad after all. I felt that if we made it though the next summer and got into the fall months, we could be secure, at least for another winter. I could not imagine anyone having to move in the middle of a harsh Michigan winter with the subzero weather we had been having for the last several years. I was wrong!

In January I received a letter saying I was three months behind in my rent. They claimed I had not paid during the months of July, August, and September. I was shocked and thought, "Isn't it really strange that they should wait until January if I had not paid for three months in the summer?" I went straight to my desk, and fortunately I found the three canceled checks immediately. I didn't trust letting those checks out of my hands, so I carried them down to their office and had them make copies. Nothing else was said.

The following month, on an icy cold February day with no advance warning, a realtor appeared at my door. It was one of my neighbors, and she had a prospective buyer accompanying her. She was there to show the house! Now I was really shaken, and all I could do was pray that we could stay until spring. I began to feel I had to buy a home, because otherwise we would always be subject to the whim of a landlord. A couple of months later, I learned that I needed to go in for major surgery that entailed a week's stay in the hospital. Again I relied on the law, which prevented a landlord from evicting a person who was ill until they had been released from the doctor's care. I told the real estate office that if they were going to do anything, they needed to do it right away before I went in for surgery, because after I had surgery, I would not be able to move for a couple of months.

Since Martha was seventeen and Kay was fourteen, I felt that it would be safe to allow them to come home after school and then go next door to our wonderful neighbors, Margaret and Andy Timnick, to spend the night while I was in the hospital. Our family room had a large picture window, which made the room visible from Margaret's kitchen window. By leaving the drapes open in the afternoon, Martha and Kay could look over and see Margaret and feel quite secure as they did their homework. It seemed a good plan. However, on the very day of my surgery, the real estate people sent a whole crew of men out to the house to prune the plants, trees, and bushes and to make repairs in the basement that I had requested over a year before. It never occurred to me that they would choose the time of my surgery for repairs. Having strange men in the house when my teenaged daughters came home from school was totally unacceptable. My neighbors called the sheriff but were told that because repairs were authorized by the homeowner, there was nothing they could do. All too soon my experience of becoming single had joined with Mary Kay's experiences of discrimination based on gender.

As Mary Kay heard stories of what continued to happen to her people, her passion to improve the financial ability of women remained white hot. Although my situation was not new to Mary Kay, it added to those she had personally faced. Intimate knowledge of the formidable odds facing women had been gleaned from a sales career that spanned twenty-five years and continued after opening her own company. She had chosen a career in sales because traditionally the field of sales was kinder to women in terms of equal pay for men and women. However, she discovered, as in the case of her young assistant, that working harder was of little avail. She found that no matter the ability, no matter the seniority, top management positions were off limits to her. She was told, "A man has a family to support." To which she responded, "What did they think my three children were?"

When she established her own company, Mary Kay set about to correct this, because she believed with all her heart that God does not value the female brain less than a male's brain. A female brain is certainly worth more than fifty cents on the dollar. This sort of injustice fanned the dream into a white-hot passion, a magnificent obsession to offer women a chance to provide financially for themselves and their children. I was one of the recipients of this dream, and it could not have come at a better time.

Since becoming a single mom, I realized that I had become exactly the type of woman Mary Kay had in mind when she founded her woman-friendly company. I was the typical woman of that era who did not have credit in her own name. Even though I paid cash for everything, I realized I could never own a home unless I established credit. Because Mary Kay had to deal with similar issues, she was a great role model.

She also realized that too many women lacked the necessary confidence in their own abilities that they were unable to take advantage of the opportunities her company offered. Thus, her second passion became to give women a vision of their own incredible value and build belief in their God-given abilities. These were the twin passions that drove her into becoming, in the minds of many of us, the most important American woman to have lived in the twentieth century.

This second passion was also aimed squarely at where I lived, for I was lacking in self-confidence and filled with fear. The memory I have of sitting in my living room in a state of near panic is still vivid. After the girls were in bed, I would look around the room and fill my mind with frightful images. Terrified, I thought, "What will happen if something happens to me? I have two daughters who are completely dependent on me. The rent would not get paid, the lights would go out, and there would be no food in the refrigerator."

I remember the evening I drove across town for a four-dollar sale so that I could have those dollars to buy food for our evening meal. Everything was a cash transaction, for I had no credit card. In purchasing only what could be covered by the cash in my purse, I sometimes embarrassed my daughters by buying only a dollar's worth of gas to keep the car running. Fortunately, gas was cheap.

People made statements to me like, "Without your husband you will starve to death," which only fueled my feelings of inadequacy! They certainly didn't do much to reassure me. But thanks to my parents' help and Mary Kay's dream company, that didn't happen!

Mary Kay watched what criticism over one mistake did to a very capable and talented woman whose career was destroyed by it. She knew that criticism and fear were the enemies, and she was determined to replace them with praise, love, inspiration, and courage. I desperately needed someone to believe in *me*.

Mary Kay taught us to "look for something good to appreciate in each person you meet, and then tell them about it. Give a sincere compliment." Since then I have often seen just how powerful a few simple words can be. One such occasion occurred in Dallas at an annual seminar when I had a casual conversation with a consultant in an elevator at my hotel. Since I had dozens of conversations during the seminar, I didn't think about it again. A year later, that same young lady came up to me and thanked me profusely for the words I spoke to her in the elevator the year before. It was a humbling experience, for I was left standing there thinking, "What in the world could I possibly have said in that short time that would make such a difference in her life that she would remember for a year?"

This story illustrates Mary Kay's point that you can literally praise a woman to success. From her years of selling through home parties, she came to realize that "women are starved for sincere appreciation and praise. A woman can live a month on one compliment. For many women, graduation from high school was the last time they got any recognition."

I remember another occasion when I was still living in Dallas where I arrived at a home to find that my hostess was in a terrible mood. Her mood did not change at all during the class. I knew I had done nothing to cause her displeasure; nevertheless, it was an uncomfortable situation. At that point, my only desire was to get out of there as fast as possible. But I remembered that Mary Kay had told us that unhappy people are the most in need of kindness, so I tried to be kind to her throughout the entire class. When I got home, I sent the usual thank-you note for inviting me into her home. Nine months later I got a call from this same woman. I remembered exactly who she was because the class stood out in my memory as my most discouraging class. She told me she had spent the entire day looking for my phone number. She had even called the company and asked who had come to her home, but the company had no way of knowing. They offered to give her the name of someone else, but she told them she didn't want anyone else. When she finally found my number and called, she acted as if I was her long lost friend and placed an order for the basic five-step skin care. Later, she did, indeed, become my friend and faithfully placed large orders until I moved to Michigan.

By teaching us to look for ways to give genuine compliments to others, Mary Kay helped us take the focus off ourselves. This in itself helped people like me to feel better about themselves because of the positive responses the compliments elicited. She encouraged us to take praise into our homes and praise our children and husbands in the same way.

Mary Kay created a whole new corporate structure for the American workplace. Emphasizing the practice of the Golden Rule to guide every practice in business and personal life gave rise to what Mary Kay called "the Mary Kay go-give spirit." In this culture, things like gossip, pettiness, criticism, and backstabbing found no place. In a business where each person had their own ladder to success, there was no reason to be jealous of the success of others. Each person could promote herself according to her own achievements without waiting for someone to die or retire. Cooperation and sharing were the natural outgrowth of weekly sales meetings, which were created to be a safe environment for women to gain new skills, new friendships, and self-confidence. Mary Kay turned individual women who had never been a part of any team into team players who joyously applauded each other's successes.

Mary Kay was liberal with her praise for me. A letter I received from Mary Kay in February 1975 is an example of the way she encouraged and reinforced my efforts. In it she referred to challenges that she knew I had faced in the previous year. The spring of 1974 had begun with an illness that almost killed my father, who was then taking care of my blind, semi-invalid mother. His illness was followed by major surgery for me, Martha's high school graduation, and then the finalization of my divorce. Here is a section of the letter just as she wrote it, caps and all:

> *I WAS THRILLED with your letter—THRILLED to know you have picked up the pieces of your life—and instead of being worn down by all the obstacles you have overcome, you have been polished up! I am reminded that a diamond is just a hunk of coal—just highly polished. If you will show me someone who has made it BIG, I can almost always show you someone who shouldn't have made it at all. I think that with all your problems you have overcome, that is your case. You DID make it, and now you have your life in the proper perspective. You will go ON to greater and greater things.*

Mary Kay wanted all of her people to be as excited about life as she was. She was constantly modeling for us the type of behavior she wanted exhibited in our lives. Her leader's heart was well demonstrated in the letters she wrote.

5 The Look of a Golden Rule Company

It took a long time to expunge the skeptic in me. I eventually found the answer to my question of what a company that operated under the principle of the Golden Rule would actually look like: it is a life-enhancing, life-affirming, stimulating, invigorating way to live and conduct business. In light of all the front-page news involving business scandals, today's corporations would do well if they emulated the way Mary Kay established her business; it could be the smart thing to do.

However, Mary Kay didn't do it because she considered it expedient; she did it because that was who she was. Despite all of the accolades accorded to Mary Kay Inc.'s brilliant marketing plan, what may not be recognized is that the plan will not achieve lasting success without the principles. Mary Kay's business was built firmly upon the enduring principles of faith and integrity—principles that have stood the test of time. This idea of running a business according to the principle of the Golden Rule is now so much associated with Mary Kay's company that we might not recognize how amazing the concept really is. Some companies have tried to copy Mary Kay's methods but have really lacked an understanding of all the ramifications involved. Even today, it remains a revolutionary idea! It requires integrity on every level. This success didn't just happen because Mary Kay announced it. It took a lot of work and determination on her part to make it happen.

So, what does such a company look like? Her audacious dream required consultants to relate to one another in unprecedented ways. Although they are in fact competitors for the *same* cosmetic market, they do not treat each other as such. Instead, just as she pictured, consultants share ideas with each other like buddies, applaud each other's successes like sisters, and respect each other's customers as if they were partners. What Mary Kay asked her consultants to do is to operate as if their competitors (the other consultants) were their dearest friends. She envisioned a woman-friendly company in which women would not only operate unselfishly with each other but also go beyond that to treat each other with extravagant generosity. Her goal was for her company to have a uniquely positive character, designed according to the way she would like to have been treated by the companies for whom she had worked. That is exactly what she ultimately achieved.

In keeping with this cooperative environment, Mary Kay encouraged the free exchange of ideas. Her philosophy was, "If you have an idea and I have an idea and we each keep our idea to ourselves, all we have is one idea. However, if you have an idea and I have an idea and we share our ideas, we now have *two* ideas."

One thing I could always count on was that Mary Kay would listen to my ideas with a sympathetic ear. As we shared ideas, Mary Kay not only accorded respect for our brainchild, she led the applause. This had the added value of giving me the feeling of ownership in the company. To her, there were no dumb ideas. She was extremely open to considering and accepting ideas, regardless of the achievement level of the associate who originated it. This was part of the genius of her leadership.

Ann Sullivan, who rose to the top position of national sales director, introduced one such idea. Ann started recognizing consultants in her unit once they had started their team by sponsoring at least three consultants in the business. And she made that recognition of their achievement lasting by having them wear a red jacket, white blouse, and black skirt to all Mary Kay functions. Mary Kay adopted Ann's idea and made it nationwide, and now you see women in red jackets at all Mary Kay events.

The application of the Golden Rule to every phase of the business resulted in a very safe environment. Whenever we came into contact with another consultant's customer in the course of doing business, we had a hands-off policy. We were taught that one of the first things we should ask a prospective customer is, "Do you have a Mary Kay consultant from whom you purchase your cosmetics?" If she does, we encourage her to be loyal to her original consultant. We do *not* try to interest her in switching consultants. Even if she is ready to buy additional product on the spot, we explain that in Mary Kay we don't want to take each other's customers. This way when consultants gather for meetings there are no hurt feelings.

Mary Kay eliminated territories in her plan. She realized that people relate differently to various personalities and have strong ties to people beyond their neighborhoods. For this reason, she felt that territories made no sense and restricted a woman's ability to expand her business. She often told us, "One of you might find it possible to recruit one of my very own neighbors when that person might never recruit with me."

Although her primary focus was to create a structure without territories that would benefit her consultants, her plan turned out to be fantastic for business also. In fact, elimination of territories proved to be a brilliant marketing tool.

Since as a consultant I was not restricted to my city, I was able to introduce my good friend Audrey from Philadelphia into Mary Kay when she visited me in Dallas on her way to vacation in Mexico. I was also motivated to introduce the Mary Kay business to relatives and friends anywhere in the United States. It made sense and good business to have the added joy of being able to work with people I cared about, even if they didn't live in my city. Later it also made it possible for me to relocate. When I started my business in Dallas, I didn't plan to move, but a little over two years later I moved to Michigan. I retained the team members I had established in Dallas and retained my affiliation with my original unit and director.

With benefits like these, the company grew without costly investments in advertising. The money that might have been used for advertising was used for other company programs that benefited the sales force. The amazing growth literally resulted from one woman telling another woman. Mary Kay's description of effective communication became "telegraph, telephone, and tell-a-woman." She was convinced that "tell-a-woman" was by far the most effective way.

The nine consultants who originally joined Mary Kay in opening the company were Mary Kay's personal friends or former business associates. In the beginning, because of their enthusiasm and close relationship to Mary Kay, a Golden Rule culture came about quite naturally. As these women sponsored new people, they also brought friends and relatives into the business, people with whom they enjoyed associating. It remained easy to transfer this "go-give spirit," as Mary Kay called it, to these second-generation consultants. The test came as the company began to spread out away from the central core of consultants who were in Mary Kay's direct sphere of influence.

After the number of consultants increased beyond the number Mary Kay could personally manage, she began to appoint successful consultants who were excellent in sales and team building to become directors of their own teams. The unique company climate operated extremely well as long as new consultants were closely tied into contacts with the Dallas-based units. It was inevitable that as more and more miles separated new team members, women would join who were not deeply committed to the Mary Kay way of doing business. It followed that those who had not been immersed in a Golden Rule culture would begin their business without an allegiance to any business other than their own. And as more and more consultants became scattered across the country, a new challenge arose. This wonderful growth left many individuals without access to local training and support because they lived in areas other than those of their sponsoring unit.

In Mary Kay's system, all sales directors were expected to welcome women from other units into their training and sales meetings, even though this would never benefit them financially. The monetary benefit would go to the other unit director living in a different part of the country. This defied standard business practice. Conducting business according to the Golden Rule did not come naturally just because a woman joined Mary Kay. It had to be taught and caught.

Normally, business people expect compensation for developing sales personnel, and they certainly don't provide free assistance to their competition! The assumption of Mary Kay's system was that this would be a reciprocal arrangement. Other directors elsewhere would extend the same courtesy to their people. This concept of doing business was unlike any other business that I knew. Adherence to the Golden Rule was paramount if this system was to prevail.

Nevertheless, it is not surprising that Mary Kay began to hear of cities where consultants affiliated with out-of-town units were not being welcomed and trained. Not everyone was implementing the go-give spirit. These new people had to be encouraged and trained. In practice, the go-give spirit was beginning to break down. A search for a remedy was undertaken. In order for individuals to succeed, the company was finding it was vital for consultants to be plugged into a local director's group.

Finally, after her business advisors insisted, Mary Kay reluctantly agreed to institute a "closed city" plan in order to meet the critical need for training and give individuals the help they needed. This meant that each city or town was assigned a quota of directors based on the population of the area. If a city's quota of directors was four, then the city was closed when that number of directors was met. Consultants who lived outside the city could no longer sponsor someone living inside that city. Consultants who had been sponsored by someone outside the city were taken from that person and placed in one of the four local directors' units. This spelled the end of the "no territories" policy. It also spelled trouble for the company. While it solved one problem, it created a bigger problem. When consultants could no longer receive credit for sponsoring people outside their area, recruiting was significantly reduced. The company began to realize that the closed city policy wasn't going to work. Mary Kay returned to the no territories policy and renewed efforts to make the go-give spirit work all over the country. Mary Kay announced a new prestigious award, Miss Go-Give, which was to be awarded annually to the most outstanding director of the year who went beyond the call of duty to welcome and assist consultants who were not their own. Mary Kay promoted this award as the top award the company could bestow. She considered it more important than earning a Cadillac.

Still, there were problems. During times of phenomenal growth in various parts of the country, the go-give culture became particularly vulnerable. Mary Kay continued to hear that consultants in some areas were not being trained and nurtured. Fortunately, this was not the way the majority of directors acted. Many directors across the country have worked hard to maintain Mary Kay's philosophy of the Golden Rule.

The Michigan area produced a couple of outstanding directors who played a key role. The first is Doris Gessner, who recognized the problem and decided to act. Doris had come into my unit in Michigan and in a short time went on to become Michigan's third director. Doris is the kind of person who does not need to be prompted to remember to act with integrity in her daily life. She, like many other Mary Kay people, had acquired a feeling of ownership in the company. Because there were consultants in Detroit but no directors to hold sales meeting closer than Ann Arbor, Doris decided to add an extra meeting to her crowded schedule. She drove into the city and held a meeting for consultants, all at her own expense, though she had no special connection or longstanding friendship with the consultants or their directors. A couple of consultants from director Rubye Lee's unit in Atlanta, who attended Doris' meetings, had goals to become directors themselves. Rubye's goal was to advance to the highest position in Mary Kay, that of national sales director. If her two consultants became directors, Rubye would achieve her goal, because two more directors was all Rubye needed.

As Mary Kay continued to wrestle with the problem of providing nurturing to all consultants, there were reports of a problem in one of the rapidly growing states, so Mary Kay made arrangements to travel to that area to be the featured speaker at the debut of these new sales directors. Since this area was within driving distance for Doris, she decided to take advantage of the opportunity to see Mary Kay. While attending the event, Doris happened to overhear a conversation between two brand new consultants who were complaining that they had not received any training and felt very lost. Doris realized that this was something that Mary Kay would want to hear.

Mary Kay stayed to shake hands, talk to, and have pictures taken with every person who stood in line to greet her at the end of the evening. Doris waited. Although it had been a long evening, Mary Kay sat down with Doris to listen to what she had to say. Doris shared what she had overheard that evening and discovered that this was the very reason that Mary Kay had decided to visit the area. Mary Kay and the corporate staff had been hearing similar reports. She asked Doris to think about what could be done and said, "If you come up with a good solution, I want to hear about it."

Doris did think about it, but she couldn't come up with the big idea that Mary Kay was searching for, so she turned her attention to what she could do in her area to make consultants from all units feel welcome. The thought occurred to her to design a Certificate of Adoption to present to those who attended her meetings but were not a part of her unit. Since she didn't see this as *the* solution that Mary Kay was looking for, she didn't mention it. Doris began having a little ceremony and presenting each with a certificate, which she hoped would help them feel they had a home away from home and could expect to be treated the same as if they were her own people.

Soon Mary Kay called Doris and said, with mock severity, "Doris, I thought I told you that if you came up with an idea to solve the problem we were discussing the last time we talked, you were supposed to call me with it!"

Doris replied, "Yes, you did ask me to do that, Mary Kay, but I figured this wasn't that big." However, Mary Kay felt as if Doris had offered the company something it very much needed. She asked for a copy and put the Adoption Certificate into company-wide use. For her selfless acts, Doris was awarded the Miss Go-Give award at the annual seminar by the company president, Larry Harley.

A second key player was director Fran Cikalo. Even before Fran became Michigan's first national sales director, she led the way in creating the warm climate of fun and inclusion that became Michigan's legacy in the Mary Kay world. Those of us who were Michigan's first directors had become friends. We had directors' meetings in each other's homes in the Detroit area. We supported each other as we grew. Fran was determined that the loyalty the first directors felt for each other should become the standard for all the Michigan directors who would follow.

Fran has an enormous talent for organizing and putting on

workshops and seminars. She put these skills to work to benefit all of us. She got her whole family involved in the preparations. To keep costs down in the early days, Fran's family provided the food for all those attending. Behind the scenes, her husband Jim stepped in to handle emergences like running out of food at some of the first events. Without the backing of the company, she went out on a financial limb, signing contracts to rent Detroit's convention center and ballrooms in the Westin Hotel on Detroit's waterfront. She negotiated special room rates at the hotel for attendees. In addition, she copied Mary Kay's high hostess events and organized huge hostess contests at Detroit's Convention Center, where real jewelry, furs, and appliances were awarded to top hostesses who were responsible for hundreds of dollars worth of sales for their consultants. Fran's events even rivaled the lavish Dallas contests. They were a tremendous help in motivating consultants and directors in the area. Like consultants and directors from outlying areas, we would drive in to take advantage of what Fran made available.

When Fran became Michigan's first national director, she was determined that every Michigan director be welcoming and helpful to all Mary Kay people. Her annual January Jamborees attracted twenty-five hundred consultants and directors. I believe that Fran's efforts benefited more Mary Kay people than any other person in the state. They provided knowledge, inspiration, fun, and also the tools to develop profitable businesses.

Exceptional acts of unselfishness keep multiplying across the Mary Kay organization. Today, monthly Miss Go-Give awards are presented in each of the five divisions of Mary Kay. Acting in this spirit has become a way of life for thousands upon thousands of Mary Kay consultants and directors, as women are continuing to be taught how to soar.

Mary Kay applied Golden Rule integrity to everything. This included our products and the way they were marketed. It was demonstrated in the way she watched over the development of the products. She was appalled by a company that continued to market products even after they were mandated to carry a label stating that their product could prove hazardous to the consumer's health. At the time I joined Mary Kay, the night cream contained ammoniated mercury, a healing agent. During that period, hospitals used it to clear rashes on the skin of newborn babies, so it seemed perfectly safe to be used in our night cream if it was being used on delicate infant skin. It needed to be handled with great care, however, because certain people had adverse reactions to it. Mary Kay therefore made sure that her consultants were carefully instructed to make a patch test on each new customer's skin on the delicate tissue inside the crease of the elbow. If that area turned pink, we removed the tiny amount of cream immediately. That customer was then given a night cream without the ammoniated mercury. When additional research came in with new disturbing questions about ammoniated mercury, she reacted swiftly to eliminate it completely from the line.

Mary Kay also made sure that the company stayed abreast of the latest research in skin care. To ensure that there would be a reliable source of such information, she made grants to schools of dermatology so that our skin care program could provide *the best* to the consumer. No outside watchdog group ever had to convince Mary Kay to do the right thing. She wanted to be sure that her products would do no harm to anyone's skin. She acted in advance of the FDA, who later mandated that ammoniated mercury be removed from all cosmetics. Mary Kay was determined to do good rather than harm.

Our product guarantee is not a limited one; it is a 100 percent guarantee of satisfaction. During a question and answer period with directors, one woman asked about the return policy for used cosmetics. "Mary Kay, how about a product that has been half used up?" Mary Kay answered with a smile, "Yes, even if it contains such a tiny amount around the rim that you have trouble seeing it. Yes, and do it with a smile! The point is that she, your customer, is *unhappy*, and I don't want you to have unhappy customers. That woman will probably go around and tell all her friends how nice we were to her."

Mary Kay's word was her bond, so she wanted her representatives to be truthful and accurate about our products and company. This was important to me. I appreciated Mary Kay's attitude, because my father had valued the same principles in dealing with people. I had been brought up with those principles. Daddy stated it this way: "It is better to be the person that is being wronged than the person committing the wrong." Money was not a primary motivator for Mary Kay, so as she became increasingly successful, greed did not entangle her life.

Her faith in God influenced everything she did. Since Mary Kay's faith was not a Sunday-only faith, it made a difference in her business. I was not in the company very long when I learned that from the beginning she had taken God as her senior partner in the business. She did not take him as her junior partner. This would have allowed her to make the decisions and then ask for God's blessings. Neither did she take him as an equal partner. She took him as her senior partner, the controlling partner. She wanted God to be the guiding force in the decisions and the direction of the company. Living out this decision would become the ingredient that would make and keep the company unique. This is the secret that many of the companies that have tried to copy her business plan have failed to embrace.

As conscientious as she was, she didn't take credit for all these right decisions. Rather than become proud of the way the company did business, she was humble. When she reflected on the way the company had grown, she spoke with a sense of awe. I often heard Mary Kay say, "Although we have extraordinary people working for us in Mary Kay, no one is smart enough to have made all those right decisions that we have made through the years." She credited this to the guidance of her senior partner.

From the first day, Mary Kay felt God's touch in the decisions that were made regarding her new business. Many times I have heard her relate a story about the guidance she received regarding personnel when she opened the company. For instance, she turned down one highly qualified and enthusiastic salesperson who was eager to sell for the company, even though it didn't make sense to turn away help that she desperately needed in launching the company. Something didn't seem right about that person, so she refused the help. A few months later, that person made headlines after being charged with a felony. An association with this person could have proved disastrous for the fledgling company.

Integrity flowed as a product of faith and permeated every corner of Mary Kay's life. It was a cornerstone of her character. Therefore, she did not tolerate questionable business practices. Her kind of integrity went beyond consideration of what was legal. If an idea did not meet her standard surfaced during a company board meeting, her face would get a look that told those who knew her well that she was not pleased with the direction of the planning. And if one of her lawyers reassured her by saying that what they were discussing was legal, her response was, "It may be legal, but it's not right! And we aren't going to do it." And she didn't!

In her speech and in her letters, the heart of this leader's faith in God came through in a very natural way. This view of her company was expressed many times and in many ways. In a letter she sent me dated April 15, 1977, she wrote,

> *I truly believe that Mary Kay Cosmetics is a vehicle that God is using to make this a better world, and as we touch people's lives and enrich them, we are truly working for Him.*

This was a thought that she expressed time and again throughout her lifetime. She wrote to me in a letter in August 1989,

> *Do what you can do and expect God to do what He can do— MIRACLES! He is more than enough to make you more than you thought you could be.... Please know that you are in my heart and in my prayers.*

Corporate responsibility extended into areas of safety and cleanliness as well. In the beginning there were no disposable products and brushes. Some of the veteran consultants now joke that we weren't aware of the germ theory at that time. This is not true! It was unthinkable to Mary Kay that we would represent her without using clean, safe products. Mary Kay instructed us in a routine to sanitize everything we used. At the time, we had no disposable product from which to demonstrate, so we used the actual product. This cleaning process took an hour to complete. It was thorough, effective, and safe but very labor intensive. "How to clean your sales case" was a standard part of the first consultant orientation classes that I attended.

Mary Kay's personal practice of the Golden Rule was not limited to her own organization. As she related to and interacted with those with whom Mary Kay Cosmetics did business, she showed them the same respect that she wanted for herself. She rejoiced in their successes. She was never so focused on building her own company that she failed to see the needs of others around her. This prompted her to reach out her hand of friendship and help to other business people. Zig Ziglar credits Mary Kay with helping him become successful. From the first time she heard Zig speak, she was impressed with what he had to offer to his audiences. Since she was not selfish with her success, she tried to take as many people with her as she could. Zig developed a six-hour program devoted to providing inspiration and motivation for people in Mary Kay. He used stories of many consultants and directors as illustrations. Directors all across the country invited him into their areas. I booked him twice for the Lansing area. He gave a full six-hour, life-changing presentation to Mary Kay groups as small as fifty people.

Since I knew Mary Kay was willing to help other business people, I introduced her to people from Michigan who could possibly be mutually beneficial. In the spring of 1972, Mary Kay graciously met with a lady from Michigan that I introduced to her, and although Mary Kay could not use the woman's services, she wrote me a note saying how much she enjoyed the meeting.

Excellence was her standard in all things, and this included the entertainment provided for the lavish award nights at the annual seminars. When Mary Kay gave gifts or celebrated the achievements of her sales force, she selected the top of the line. She wanted great entertainment for the awards evening, so a top performer was engaged each year. She believed people could have a wonderful time without indulging in crude or offensive behavior, so before each performer was booked, he or she was given the ground rules: no suggestive or off-color material allowed.

Outstanding shows were presented each year and always lived up to Mary Kay's expectations, with one exception, which occurred when a performer was booked a few years later for a second performance. Perhaps it was assumed that he remembered the rules. But apparently he did not remember, because once on stage, he launched into off-color jokes. After my initial surprise, I turned my attention to Mary

Kay, who was seated in her box at the side of the stage. I wondered how she was reacting. One look and I could tell she was furious. She began to pace back and forth as she talked to assistants. The performance was stopped. The curtain came down, and the act was not resumed until he agreed to apologize to the audience and, in Mary Kay's words, "clean up his act."

Mary Kay felt extremely responsible for all the women who attended the seminar. She set about to change the perception of conventions from a party image where alcohol flowed freely to one where families could feel safe in sending their daughters, moms, sisters, aunts, or grandmothers. As soon as our conventions became too large to be accommodated in one hotel, Mary Kay started providing continuous bus service between the convention hotels and the convention center. She did not want women to be walking alone in unfamiliar cities. And even though it is enormously expensive, she provided the bus service at no charge so that someone short on money would not put herself at risk by walking. Ever mindful of the cost to participants, she also included breakfast and lunch in the price of registration so that the seminar would be affordable for all. One thing she did *not* provide was alcohol: no champagne, no wine, not even at awards banquets. Each year she made one request of us, which was that we stay out of bars and refrain from drinking during Mary Kay conventions and events. She made learning fun without the added risk of alcohol-related accidents.

Even brief associations with Mary Kay Inc. proved life enhancing for so many people. As I come into contact with former consultants, many have made it a point to tell me that without the things they learned in Mary Kay, they would not have had the skills or the courage to achieve the success they attained in their current life situation.

Within the first five years of founding the company, Mary Kay was already envisioning her company reaching into the lives of women of the future, to a time when she would no longer be at the helm of the company. She told us it was up to her directors to make certain that the core values remained the same. I remember responding with a determination to become a director so that I could help to keep the company headed in the same direction.

The passions of her life grew from the original two to four. The first was her determination to provide economic opportunity for women, the second was to develop women's confidence in their own abilities, the third was to find a cure for cancer, and the fourth was to end domestic violence against women and children. All four strongly affected me.

The heart of this great leader became greatly troubled when she began to recognize that something deadly was attacking her beloved "Mary Kay daughters," as she affectionately called her directors and consultants. Breast cancer began to rear its ugly head. Some of her much-loved sales force died of cancer. When Rena Tarbet, the queen of sales for the entire company, became involved in a life-and-death battle to survive the cancer that was ravaging her body, the fight to eliminate breast cancer took center stage in Mary Kay's heart. A few years later, Mary Kay's beloved husband, Mel, died of lung cancer. She was never one to shrug her shoulders and say, "There is nothing that can be done." Instead, her hatred of cancer propelled her into a fight to fund research for a cure and education for prevention.

In 1963, when the company was founded, there were no public discussions of domestic violence, just as in the case of breast cancer. Animal rights advocates were the first to recognize and take action on behalf of abused women. They expanded their endeavors and were the first to introduce shelters for battered women to our country.

Although domestic violence has existed for centuries, it has lived a shadowy existence largely hidden from public view, like an ugly family secret. Women suffered it in secret and endured it in silence, covering it up with clothing and makeup. In the event that it was noticed, it was explained away as an "accident." Even when it was exposed, eyes were diverted. Often the secret only became public knowledge when it resulted in homicide. Over the years, Mary Kay came to discover that some of the women affected by this violence were our Mary Kay girlfriends. Mary Kay became increasingly aware of this clandestine menace as she listened to the stories of more and more women she loved and cared for, and she became dedicated to breaking the silence.

Like Mary Kay, I got an intimate view of domestic violence through the people I met as consultants and directors. My business associate and good friend Lela Eaton gave me my first glimpse. After I sponsored Lela into Mary Kay, I learned Lela's story. Her daughter had been murdered by the daughter's husband, leaving her daughter's children to be reared by Lela and her husband. Several years later there was another case of violence affecting one of my consultants. It was Mary Kay herself who received the news first and told me of the murder-suicide of one of my Lansing area consultants, her husband, and her son. I added my own personal tragic experience in 1977 when my daughter Martha disappeared.

6 The Heart of a Leader When Her People Face Violence

Mary Kay's knowledge of violence grew because of my daughter's tragedy. Mary Kay's personal experience with violence was limited to one experience. When Mary Kay lived on a major thoroughfare in Dallas, her house was broken into while she was home. Though she was bound, gagged, and robbed, she managed to hobble out her front door in her nightgown to get help from her next-door neighbor. To add to the indignity she suffered, the front of her gown came apart in her struggle to free herself. It certainly was a harrowing experience to face intruders in the security of her own home.

I brought a whole new level of violence to Mary Kay's attention as a result of what took place on New Year's Eve in 1976. The scene early that evening in the kitchen of my home in the peaceful community of East Lansing, home of Michigan State University, gave no hint of impending violence. My older daughter, Martha, came downstairs into the kitchen to kiss me good-bye before she headed out the door to baby sit. She left home with her former fiancé, Don Miller. Don had insisted on driving her to baby sit for friends that both he and Martha knew. Two days earlier, however, she had broken their engagement, but he had talked her into remaining "just friends."

We could never have imagined how dangerous that simple decision to remain friends was. After all, he was no stranger. He was, in fact, a neighbor, a brother of one of Martha's friends. He had attended the same high school and even went to the same church. I thought I had every reason to believe that he was a safe person.

Don later said that he brought Martha home that night and then returned to his home. We knew he lied, however, because Martha never returned. My world came apart that day, and a frantic search began, a search that lasted into the third year after my daughter's disappearance. Because we had served as Methodist missionaries in Pakistan with a large community of Americans, we knew people all across the United States. Therefore, part of the search involved contacting every person known to Martha in every state in the country in hopes that she had been able to escape whatever danger she had faced on New Year's Eve. We desperately hoped that she had contacted someone who might give her a safe shelter. Naturally, that meant contacting Mary Kay. Since we had lived in Dallas and Martha had gone to school there, I asked Mary Kay for help in getting the word out around the Dallas area. Mary Kay told me, "We have one person on staff here that has a good working relationship with a local reporter, so possibly he can get the reporter to get the word out about Martha because she was a former Dallas resident."

Obviously, at first I was consumed with rescuing Martha and fought the thought that she had been killed. I was comfortable telling Mary Kay that finding Martha and protecting Kay were my priorities and that my business came in a distant third place. She agreed. I admitted that I was terrorized by the possibility that whoever was responsible for Martha's disappearance would also come after Kay.

I knew I had to stay sane to enable me to assist in finding Martha and protect Kay. The lesson Zig Ziglar had taught me at one of my first seminars about controlling my own thoughts was a lifesaver in my situation. "Stop!" I would often command my brain. "Don't go there!" Over and over I pulled my thoughts away from the brink of madness in order to go on functioning. Sometimes it felt like I literally took my hands and placed them inside my brain in order to shift my thoughts away from the hideous images battling for my attention.

The weekly sales meetings that I continued to conduct provided a little oasis of refreshment. I insisted that during those hours nothing about my circumstances be mentioned. I knew my consultants cared.

There was plenty of time away from the meeting for consultants to run by my home, call on the phone, or send cards. All that would have been accomplished if someone had expressed sympathy during a meeting would have been for me to dissolve into a pool of tears—and I had cried enough already! The one thing I couldn't quite manage was to sing songs. With my consultants before me, however, I could concentrate on them and on their business needs. For that brief time, I didn't have to struggle so hard to control my thoughts.

The company has a director's only leadership conference once a year. It is a mixture of information and motivation, with a glimpse into the new products and events planned for the coming year. At the leadership conference in Chicago six weeks after Martha's disappearance, Mary Kay requested that I come out of the general assembly to meet with her. She spent the entire morning sitting beside me, sometimes with her arm around me, listening and offering words of comfort. She shared how she had gotten through some of her own hard times and encouraged me to continue what I had been doing, to go on working when time was available for work in order to focus on brighter things when I could. She said she had done the same during difficult times in her life.

During the agonizing days, weeks, and months that followed, months that turned into a year, then two, and then three, Mary Kay kept up with what was going on with us. That fall, Mary Kay and Mel came to Michigan and had all the Michigan directors and their husbands meet her for dinner at the Greenfield Village Inn Restaurant in Dearborn, Michigan. As Michigan directors, we wanted to show off Michigan's unique contribution to the Mary Kay world: the Pink Cadillac. That afternoon, sales director Fran Cikalo had arranged for Mary Kay to tour the plant where the Cadillac was manufactured.

Mary Kay's visit provided something that I could look forward to. At that time, there were few directors in the state. The small intimate dinner gave me a chance to enjoy being in Mary Kay's presence. Being around her was always therapeutic, and I knew it would be for Kay too. Other directors were married and accompanied by their husbands, so Flo Allen, who was single, took her ninety-year-old mother. Mary Kay went out of her way to honor both and made sure that she spent some private moments with both Flo's mother and Kay. The visit was indeed a bright spot.

For a long time I had refused to change anything in Martha's room. At last I asked a friend to help me to do what needed to be done. Mary Kay approved. She wrote,

> *I was glad to hear that you had finally cleaned out Martha's room.*
>
> *Your letter made my day! How wonderful that you now can see the light at the end of the tunnel and that your world is beginning to revolve again. Sue, dear, you must for the sake of all of those who love you so much come to terms with Martha's absence as you are doing now and start to live again....*
>
> *It was wonderful seeing you and Kay while we were in Michigan, and I sensed that your life had turned around, and I'm so happy to hear it from you.*

In the months that followed, she expressed the same total disbelief and frustration that I felt toward the laws that failed to protect victims and allowed a killer to continue his reign of terror. For lack of evidence, I was forced to watch as other young women in our area disappeared. We knew that these women were also victims of Don. We just couldn't prove it. Often the laws seemed to tie the hands of the police who were there to protect us. At the beginning of the third year she wrote,

> *Bless your heart! I understand the agonies that you have gone through for two years now—and how helpless and frustrated you must feel at the inaction taken by all these well-meaning people. Surely God in His infinite mercy has heard our prayers—and surely, from the action that has been taken, something good will come of it. I know how disillusioned you must be, but please don't let that take hold of your heart—for people, unfortunately, in most cases are weak. Though they say nice things with their mouths, they sometimes do not follow up with their hands.*

As hopes of finding Martha alive faded, I became obsessed with the words spoken to me by the state forensic psychologist: "Unless the man responsible for Martha's disappearance is caught, he will escalate to even more violence." A year and a half later, his predictions came true, and more young women began to disappear. The local and regional police had been magnificent. They had poured their hearts and souls into the effort to rescue Martha, but the day came when the police had exhausted everything they knew to do. The lead detective, Lt. Tucker, apologetically told me that they were not closing the case, but they had come to the end of their leads. I understood that what he said was true. He assured me that the police would continue to check in on me from time to time, and they did.

At that point, my senior director, Idell, consulted with Mary Kay. She agreed with my director's plan for a fundraiser among the directors. The purpose of the fundraiser was to provide money to continue the search. With the help of these directors, I was able to hire a world-class detective with an impressive record of finding missing people. Mary Kay wrote, "I hope this small thing that we were able to do will in some way bring about the solution to the problem for you."

Mary Kay was a better correspondent than I, for often her letters ended with words like "Please keep in touch." I think part of my failure to communicate was because I didn't want to burden her. I was always very conscious of the enormous responsibility she carried as chairman of the board. Another part was my inability to stay focused on anything other than the case. I had such a struggle with keeping my mind away from the dark areas. However, Mary Kay never made me feel guilty for not writing more often. She was just concerned, as her letter of November 7, 1978, shows:

Dearest Sue,

It's been so long since I've heard from you, and this morning I had the strongest feeling that I needed to talk to you. Unfortunately, I missed you on the phone—so I thought I'd drop you a note.

What has happened where Martha Sue is concerned? Has anything further been done about Donald Miller? The last I heard ... he had been arrested—and that he was also a suspect in several other cases that are pending in the Lansing area.

I think of you so often—and worry about how you are doing. Please keep in touch and let me know what the latest news might be. We love you so very much, and my greatest concern is that you are well—and that your mental attitude is all that it should be. Please write or call.

Love you!
Mary Kay

Finally, in July 1979, we found out what had happened to Martha, and we had a memorial service. Mary Kay immediately sent us a beautiful plant. At the end of the week, I received a card with Mary Kay's handwritten note:

Dearest Sue,

My heart and thoughts have been with you all week. I know that your heart has been aching—but at least now you know that what you believed all along was true. There must be some relief of a sort in that and in knowing that someone will be brought to justice for Martha's death.
God gave you still another child—and there is much to do. Lift up your eyes and your heart. May God bless you.

Lovingly,
Mary Kay

During the time that Martha was missing, Mary Kay's heart was broken again. Under a bright Texas sun, the friendly, beautiful, talented, unpredictable, and vivacious national sales director Sue Vickers, who was a particular bright spot in Mary Kay's life, was also brutally murdered. Three days before the annual seminar, Sue had gone to North Park Shopping Mall to shop for a special pair of shoes to wear. Investigators discovered and reported that when Sue came out of the mall, she couldn't remember where she had parked her Pink Cadillac. Two "nice young men" came to her assistance and told her they would drive her around the mall so that she could spot her car. Because of Sue's friendly, trusting nature, she became easy prey to men who were far from nice. Sue and her Cadillac were found after she was abducted and murdered.

In this season of wrenching pain, my faith in God sustained me, but sometimes it seemed God was silent. I wanted not only to *know* he was present, I wanted to *feel* his presence. Sometimes I felt that God was distant.♥

♥ See appendix for "Signs of Danger"

7   Dear God, Where Are You?

When I speak and do book signings, I often hear two questions: "Did Martha's disappearance cause you to go through a period of doubt or anger at God? And how did you survive?"

The first afternoon of Martha's disappearance, as the shadows began to lengthen and announce the approaching evening, I could no longer stand staying in the house. I had to join in the search, so my minister agreed to drive me. I remember searching in a deep, snow-covered, wooded park area, screaming Martha's name into the stillness. As I probed the area, too soon the fast approaching darkness of the subzero night began extinguishing the last rays of daylight. My cries were swallowed up by the thick blanket of snow. I felt no peace. I was not lifted above my agony, yet at the same time, I had this deep knowledge that God was there and that although Martha was lost to those of us who were searching, God knew exactly where she was and she was not lost to him. I turned to him, knowing that only he had the power I needed to help me. Amazingly, I realized even then that God was giving me gifts, even in the midst of all the horror.

I also had the enormous gift of friends who were *not* like the friends of Job, whose story is told in the pages of the Bible. In Job's tragedy, his friends offered no sympathy, only pious platitudes and judgment. My friends did not. They reached out to me with compassion and love. They were willing to enter my world of suffering and be with me, from simply staying with me and just being there to working beside me doing chores and even house cleaning. (Incidentally, Job's friends got it right for a week. They sat and grieved with him in silence. It was only when they started opening their mouths and spouting religious platitudes that they got it wrong. And God was not pleased.)

Yes, I was angry, very angry that my daughter had been taken, but not with God. Actually, I considered it a gift that I wasn't angry with God. I blamed the right person: the forces of evil that made Don do what he did. I was certainly angry that Don had taken my daughter. I wanted to wake him up to what he had done, but even in this I was given a gift, because, amazingly, I never hated the killer; instead I felt pity. That had to be God. I did, however, want Don stopped before any other beautiful young woman was murdered. Forgiveness, after all, does not mean you take away the consequences and expose others to a killer. Forgiveness toward Don was a pure gift, one I didn't have to struggle for. God just gave it to me so that my heart would not be poisoned.

As I reflect, I think that somehow in our society we have such pride in our intellect and social programs that we resist the idea of the reality of evil in our world. I think one of the reasons I feel a kindred spirit toward law enforcement is that they *know* that there is a real destructive force at work in our world. We can blame all sorts of other things—poverty, bad environment, intolerance, and lack of education—but in fact the blame resides in the individual heart for having chosen to do evil. Yes, God allowed our tragedy because he gave us free will, but he was not responsible for it. For God to have caused Martha's horrible death in order to somehow refine my character or the character of our family would make God into a monster. We imprison men for doing such things.

At times, we misplace our anger and direct it toward the wrong person. I choose to direct my anger toward the devil. God is for us. He sent Jesus to bring life abundantly. It is the devil who is trying to kill us.

Another gift was the ability to be able to *feel* gratitude, to recognize and appreciate the pain in other people's lives as they shared mine, and to be thankful for the help I was receiving. What I learned through my Mary Kay business had prepared me to fully experience those gifts. Without the gift of this preparation and the life skills I had acquired as a result, the gifts of thanksgiving, gratitude, and appreciation would have been significantly diminished. Our family found favor with law enforcement, the community, and even the media. I found the answer to my question about the presence of God in the gifts he imparted: his spirit within me, the eyes of friends and even strangers, the capacities to retain empathy and compassion, gratitude, and thanksgiving, and the ability to forgive.

Almost three decades later, I was made aware of an incredible act of God on my behalf. Following a phone call I made to Barb Jackson, a friend from the large prayer group I attended, on the day Martha disappeared, God gave Barb a vision of exactly what had happened to Martha but without the location. It wasn't until after *Lethal Friendship* was published that Barb told me what she had experienced following my call. She told me that as she saw the images, she screamed, "Jesus, what do you want me to do with this? I can't tell Sue." The answer came: "Pray for Sue for grace and courage." For years, Barb felt that she had to maintain silence about what she had seen. As she wept, Barb accepted that burden to pray; and from that day forward, Barb was obedient to the Lord's call with such intensity that I began to hear reports that Barb must be having a mental breakdown, because all she did was cry and pray. What a gift those prayers were, because favor was extended to me on every front and courage was there when I needed it.

During those dark days, I could feel the power of prayer. I am just humbled to know something of the horrendous burden and the cost that my friend and the others who prayed so faithfully had willingly endured for our family and me.♥

♥ See Appendix for "Handling Tragedy."

8
Life Skills Learned from Mary Kay

I have often said that Mary Kay Cosmetics is the best self-improvement course I could have ever taken and gotten paid handsomely in the process. Through it I have developed six life-enhancing skills that enrich my life in the good times and provide survival tools in the worst of times.

1. Take yourself out of the center of your universe and focus on others.

I have often told my consultants: "Unless you were a really close friend, you probably would not have liked me if you had known me before I joined Mary Kay. Because I was so shy, I appeared snobbish. I didn't talk to people. I didn't know how. My mind was constantly evaluating every comment I uttered. Since I rarely thought of something that I didn't think would sound dumb or redundant, I felt I had nothing to contribute to a conversation. I still have a vivid memory of a date I had in college. I was unaware that my date had decided to make it a double date, and when I was introduced to this sophisticated couple, I was so intimidated by them that after the hellos I couldn't think of one thing to say all evening, not even to my date. Needless to say, he never asked me out again."

Mary Kay taught me the secret of relating to other people. It was simply a matter of shifting my focus away from preoccupation with myself. From her example I learned to really listen to others. She realized people were hungry for kind words. "Remember," she said, "everyone likes to feel important. So see each person with an invisible sign around their neck that says 'Make me feel important.'" She also offered the insight that if someone treated us unkindly, more than likely it had nothing to do with us! What a difference this made. I now began to see that someone else had probably "kicked their cat" long before I was even on the scene; thus their unhappiness had nothing to do with me. This realization helped me evolve from a person who was constantly getting her feelings hurt to one to whom that rarely happens. My change came about when I actively accepted the fact that as long as I was focused on myself, I could not successfully interact with others. By concentrating on a world outside myself, I learned how to talk to virtually anyone I met. This skill would be essential when I took on the task of assisting in the apprehension and prosecution of my daughter's killer.

Occasionally a guest would arrive at one of my skin care classes with a bad attitude. After listening to her talk, I assumed that she had had a rough day at work and set about to make her feel better. I often suggested that we all give the guest a round of applause for being a good sport and coming anyway, even after having a challenging day. Then I would start clapping and keep on clapping until the others joined me. I followed this by going over to her and assuring her that we would pamper her that evening so that she would feel better. I began to instruct my consultants not to take things personally and taught them how to turn around a negative situation.

2. Show appreciation to others and develop an attitude of gratitude.

This approach is what makes Mary Kay Inc. a "feel good" type of business. I had to learn to cultivate an attitude of gratitude. Humor helped me do that. Prior to joining I had no sense of humor. I took myself very seriously and therefore approached all of life as a serious matter. I had to learn to lighten up and even learn to laugh at myself and my mistakes. I was helped to become aware that this business, after all, isn't brain surgery! In place of concentrating on one's self, Mary Kay taught us to celebrate good in other people. She was a student of the Bible, and she put into action the admonition to think about things that are pure, lovely, and of good report.

The practice of being grateful benefits our families as well as our business. I learned that the evening meal could be a time to build appreciation into the lives of my children. Having each person tell about what was the best thing about their day, or perhaps the most enjoyable or the funniest, and having the others really listen fostered positive interaction around our dinner table. The Bible talks about being kind and affectionate to one another and about encouraging one another and building each other up, but so often we fail to give voice to our kind thoughts. I learned to make a habit of giving a sincere compliment. When I did this in my sales meetings, I discovered that some women are so unaccustomed to receiving any praise that they deny or reject it. Mary Kay told us, "You need to create a climate of receptivity toward compliments. The rule is that when a compliment is addressed to you, you can respond only by saying thank you, with no words of denial." When I taught this to my consultants, I asked them to consider what a refusal to accept a compliment says to the one giving the compliment: it says, "You are wrong" or "I don't value your opinion."

I continue to see the benefits of being an encourager in my daily life. One evening, as I was preparing dinner for a small dinner party that my daughter and I were having for close friends, I began thinking about the things that I appreciated about the people who would attend. After the blessing, I suggested that we go around the table and focus on one person at a time. Then I said, "I want each of you to tell that person one thing that you appreciate about her. Since I have had time to think about this, I will go first." Months later, one of the women still remembered exactly what I said about her and told me how much it meant to her. By sharing my heart that day, I made a difference in one life and forged a deeper friendship with one of my daughter's good friends. I have found that not only does the practice of finding good in other people enrich the lives of those around you, it also reflects back and enriches your own life in the process.

Showing appreciation can even help you get out of an emotional slump. One day one of my top consultants, Sue Yelvingtong O'Neal called to ask for help in getting out of a down day. After listening to Sue, who rarely had a bad day, I suggested that she needed to do something nice for someone else. "Think about twelve people who have made a positive contribution to your life, even in some small way." After I helped her start her list, I told her, "Go to the florist and buy twelve roses; then deliver a rose to each friend and tell them you are doing it just because they are important in your life." (This was a practice I learned from my good friend Jan Williams, who is in insurance. Jan would appear occasionally at my door with a long-stemmed red rose for no reason other than that she wanted to do something nice for her clients. As you can imagine, my friend developed a successful business.) Sue bought and delivered the roses. Later she reported, "By the time I had delivered only three of the twelve roses, I was flying high! My negative mood was gone." The fragrance of the flowers lingered with her after she had given them away.

In short, I have found that when you take exclusive focus off yourself in order to appreciate another person, your situation improves. If you have cultivated the habit of a grateful heart, it will stand you in good stead, even in the worst circumstances.

3. Control your thoughts.

Because of Zig Ziglar's teaching, which I discussed in the chapter on "stinkin' thinkin'," I discovered it is possible to take your thoughts captive and that it is impossible to think two different thoughts at the same time. In this way it is possible to control your thoughts.

I must confess that in the beginning of my career I thought that "no negativity at sales meetings" was a silly rule. Only after my daughter disappeared did I realize it was of huge importance. I wrote about this in *Lethal Friendship*:

> As the area's only director, my sales meetings were packed every Monday morning. Resuming these meetings presented a challenge because Mary Kay stressed "no negativity." Before the second Monday in January, my situation was common knowledge. Obviously my circumstances were not conducive to an entirely positive meeting. The facts were like an elephant in the room too big to be ignored. … I could have

cancelled; instead I went as usual. I did change the opening, however. My first words were: "All of you know what happened on New Year's Eve and I know you care, *however*, we are trained in Mary Kay to keep sales meetings positive. That applies to me as well. So please don't talk to me about it before or during the sales meeting or even in the parking lot afterward. You can call me at home or come by the house, but at meetings let's keep it positive. As long as we are talking about business, that will give me something else to thing about for a change. This will give me a brief break."

My heart was not in anything outside the investigation. However, because I did care about the women who came to my meetings, I could carry on and rejoice in their successes. This allowed me to focus on something other than my own pain. Planning the meetings and conducting them weekly gave me a little oasis of refreshment, a time when I didn't have to struggle so hard to control my thoughts.

Later, Rene, one of my consultants who went on to become a director, shared how that example kept her in the business when she was experiencing a hard period in her life. She made the decision to continue coming to sales meeting in the midst of her unhappy time. Rene told me she knew that the sales meetings would be a safe place where she could find a brief haven of refreshment. She credits this small thing with saving her career.

To help control thoughts in times that are less than ideal, I adopted something that the author and speaker Karen O'Connor and her husband Charles practice. They have a blessing box and keep a pen and pad of paper next to it. Each time they have an answer to a prayer or experience God's special touch, they record it on one of the slips of paper and put it in the box. To refresh themselves and provide encouragement when times are trying, they take out the slips and read concrete examples of how God has been faithful in their lives. This is something that I could see Mary Kay doing.

4. Think positive thoughts.

I remember being fascinated by a major article in *Life* magazine that depicted the human body surrounded by energy fields. I was reminded of the paintings from the great artists of the Middle Ages where halos surrounded the heads of the saints. The article talked about an aura, or energy force, emitted from every human being. I learned that science has shown that the human body is made of energy fields and that this aura or energy around us can actually be photographed by special equipment.

Sometime later at a Mary Kay seminar, I saw a demonstration showing the effect of the aura of negative thoughts on a person's strength. A volunteer from the audience of several hundred directors was asked to come on stage to assist in a demonstration. This lady was told to hold out one arm and resist the pressure that was going to be applied to it. Then the speaker told us she was going to use both hands and exert all of her strength against the outstretched arm to try to push it down. At the same time, the audience was instructed to assist the volunteer by thinking positive thoughts about her. The result was that the speaker was unable to push down the arm. The volunteer was then told to leave the room and an assistant was asked to take her down the hall, far enough away so that nothing that was said in the room could be heard. The audience was then told that the experiment would be performed again but with one difference. This time we were told to think bad thoughts about the volunteer. Another person was dispatched to bring her back to the room. This time the arm fell so quickly that the lady seemed to be offering no resistance, so the demonstration was tried again and yielded the same results.

I observed what had happened, but I was not convinced that thoughts alone could have such physical consequences. So, at dinner with my consultants that evening, I decided to do my own experiment. I selected Carolyn, one of the most popular consultants at the table, asked her to stand and hold out her arm and told her I was going to attempt to push it down. I instructed everyone else to think positive thoughts about Carolyn. This was easy for the women, because they all liked her. As I expected, I was unable to push her arm down. I figured that maybe Carolyn was simply stronger than I was, and I was tempted to just stop the test at that point. Instead, I sent her across the restaurant to the ladies' room so that she could not hear, and then I instructed the consultants to think about a really awful situation, the worst they could remember, while I repeated the experiment. I really had my doubts that negative thoughts alone could produce the dramatic results I had witnessed that afternoon, but I continued nevertheless. When Carolyn returned, I told her we were going to do the experiment again and she confidently held out her arm. When I applied pressure, I was absolutely shocked at how fast her arm fell! Carolyn was also shaken, because she protested, "Let's ... let's do that again. I ... I wasn't ready." Only after we repeated the exercise and her arm again fell as fast as it had before did I appreciate the tremendous power of thoughts.

When we reflect on these phenomena, most of us can remember a time, perhaps at a lecture or a musical or theatrical performance, where the room was just electric and the performance was brilliant, and perhaps another time when the same material presented by the same performer seemed wooden and devoid of any excitement. As a speaker, I have experienced times when my audience seemed really with me and other times when my audience seemed unresponsive, no matter my effort.

An experiment along these lines was conducted on a college campus. The subject of the experiment was the effect of a negative environment on the ability and performance of one of its faculty members. One of the most effective and popular professors on campus was chosen for the research. This professor was greatly loved by his students. His courses were lively, and he held the students in rapt attention. The professor did not know he was to be the subject of this study. So, without his knowledge, his students were told that during the next class session they were to act disinterested, bored, and rude. When the class convened, there was none of the customary friendliness from the students. The professor started with his usual enthusiasm. As some of the students began to whisper to each other, the professor redoubled his efforts to reach the students but to no avail. A few stared out the window. Various students rolled their eyes; others sat with their arms folded, looking bored. As the students' act continued, the professor's speech slowed. He seemed to be having trouble expressing his thoughts and hunting for the right words. Finally, confused and bewildered, he blurted out, "What are you doing to me?" The professor was relieved to know that this was an experiment to demonstrate the power of negative energy.

5. *Keep working.*

This was the advice that Mary Kay passed on to me that day at the leadership conference in Chicago when she sat with her arm around me speaking words of comfort. And work I did. On the day that the state police, civic organizations, and all law enforcement groups in the area were conducting a foot-by-foot search of the area where Martha's clothes had been found, I was where I needed to be. While waiting for news, I chose to be surrounded by people who loved me, teaching at a scheduled workshop. This was a helpful distraction and really the right decision, because no news came that day or for months to come.

6. *Step out of your comfort zone.*

When I entered the company, I learned to do things I had never done before and never wanted to do. I had lived in the Dallas area only a couple of years when I joined Mary Kay. I needed to learn how to step out of my comfort zone and meet new people, but I did not like the prospect of rejection. Therefore, I devised a strategy to cut down on the possibility of rejection. I decided to use a two-step approach with neighbors on the adjoining street. First, I purchased pretty note cards and wrote them a note introducing myself as their neighbor and enclosed a purse-sized container of body lotion that I thought they would enjoy. I figured that neighbors are not usually rude to people who live in their neighborhood and whose children go to the same schools, and I knew if they liked the lotion, they might think that other Mary Kay products were worth trying. Also, I thought no one ever throws away a handwritten note before they at least read it. I put them in the mail, and then I made a note on my calendar to follow up with a personal phone call three days later. I wanted to allow just enough time for them to receive it and have a chance to try the lotion, but not enough time to forget they had received it. I was encouraged when my plan worked.

This small step of contacting neighbors who were strangers to me was a start in becoming willing to step out of my comfort zone. A series of small steps followed that helped prepare me to take larger steps out of my comfort zone and do other completely different things for which I had no training, such as holding a police-sponsored press conference in my living room, letting a TV crew come into my home for an interview on a few minutes notice, appearing on the nightly news, answering the phone and becoming instantly involved in a live radio interview, testifying before the Michigan House and Senate, testifying before a grand jury, and appearing on *The NewsHour with Jim Lerher*. It was literally on-the-job training when it was suggested that I lobby for the bill to enable the state to pass a law mandating the civil commitment of serial killers who were due to be released from prison. With only a few minutes of coaching, I mingled with a group of professional lobbyists in order to talk to legislators. I participated in conference panels with professional journalists, testified at a criminal arraignment, and allowed *48 Hours* to follow me around for months when they were filming a story about my daughter, even while I interacted with customers and conducted a breakfast sales meeting around a restaurant table. Because of my training, I had the courage to contact and introduce myself to a powerful, young prosecuting attorney who lived in the Detroit area, ninety miles away. A friend who was a Michigan deputy attorney general believed this attorney might be able to help get important legislation passed, even though this prosecutor was largely unknown outside the Detroit area. He suggested that I make the contact. I followed the same pattern that I used when I first stepped out of my comfort zone to introduce myself to my Dallas neighbors. I wrote this young lawyer a handwritten letter and included a newspaper article from a Detroit paper about what our group of citizens was doing to get legislation passed to protect Michigan citizens from the serial killer who was due to be released. Then I marked the date on my calendar and placed the call three days later. As a result, I enlisted the support of this young lawyer, whose name is Jennifer Granholm. After she received the Democratic nomination for attorney general, Jennifer Granholm, fulfilled her promise to me and sat beside me as we lobbied the Democratic Speaker of the House. She not only became Michigan's attorney general but has also gone on to become a two-term governor. I received her help because I learned to step out of my comfort zone.

Mary Kay also taught us the value of teamwork. She always said that the way to achieve success is this: "Help enough other people succeed and you will succeed." She also said, "You can either work hard or you can work smart." You work hard, she explained, by trying to do everything by yourself, and you work smart by involving other people.

9 We Were Not Created to Be Lone Rangers

I was slow to realize that human beings were not created to live independently from others. Instead, I bought into the idea that independence and self-reliance were the top priority. Anything less was a sign of weakness. I failed my best friend from childhood because I had not given her the confidence that I would be willing to come to her aid if she needed me. Because she was not comfortable to reach out when she was in severe pain and needed transportation to the doctor, she didn't call on me to drive her. Instead, she drove herself, relying on her four-year-old daughter to operate the accelerator and the brake pedal. I decided that many people in our Western civilization place too high a value on self-reliance and following our own agenda.

Mary Kay, however, had the wisdom to see the flaws in this way of thinking. Her experience had shown her the need to both give and receive help. It is a universal fact of the human experience. Being a student of the Bible, Mary Kay recognized the consistent emphasis on community. She often said, "The top motivator for many women is to provide a helping hand to others." She was all about fellowship and sharing. She called it team building. She was quick to remind us that we could not be a success in isolation.

It was the connectedness in this business that was responsible for outstanding growth and changes in women's lives. In times of need, we drew strength from the group. There was no feeling of using up favors when we turned to each other for assistance. I often used Mary Kay's illustration of an old preacher who taught a lesson about our need for connection by using a roaring fire to illustrate his point. Without saying a word, he took tongs and separated a brightly glowing ember from the rest of the fire. He laid it by itself on the hearth. Then in silence he watched its flame flicker, fade, and turn cold. Mary Kay's point was that just as an ember will die when separated from the other logs in the fire, our dreams would fade if we separated ourselves from others. Mary Kay certainly believed that we were not created to be Lone Rangers.

Recently, the truth of that statement jumped out at me as never before when I was reading in the second chapter of Acts about the three thousand new believers who were added to the number of Jesus's followers after Peter's address. It lists three things that the followers of Jesus did: first, "they continued steadfast in the apostles' teaching"; second, they engaged in "fellowship" and "breaking of bread"; and third, they prayed. I was shocked to see prayer listed last. Wow! That ordering made me pause and consider the implications. I don't think God wants us to pray any less, but if God ranks fellowship second, then fellowship and breaking of bread with other believers must be pretty important for his people.

Even before this dawned on me, I had always been struck by the description of the early Christians: "behold how they love one another." When I reflect on that, I realize that they would have needed a personal depth of knowledge of each other in order to care so deeply. How would it have been possible to acquire this knowledge without fellowship and breaking bread together? I started thinking about the fact that Jesus himself desired fellowship when he chose twelve disciples. He even asked three of his closest disciples to be with him in the most difficult period of his life, the night before he went to the cross.

Even though Jesus promised his followers to be with them always, there must be added power where two or three are gathered in his name, because he promised to be in their midst. Special strength, wisdom, and power must somehow appear when we are joined by others. When Jesus sent out his disciples, he sent them out two by two, not individually. There has been ample proof of the power of community exhibited through the ages in the lives of his followers who gather together.

One example in today's world comes from former Democratic Congressman Tony Hall. In an address to La Jolla Community Church on December 9, 2007, Tony told us that as he traveled to trouble spots in the Middle East to have meetings with the religious leaders as an envoy for Secretary of State Condoleezza Rice, there were beginning to be some breakthroughs with centuries-old adversaries. Tony believed the reason for these successes was that he never traveled alone on these vital assignments. He always traveled with a good friend who prayed while Tony met with various leaders. Tony said, "As a congressman I have been a part of writing and signing treaties which haven't changed things, but with this approach of traveling with a prayer partner, I have seen some real miracles take place."

This insight about the power that lies in fellowship with others brought to mind the stories of two very different churches. A woman who has given me permission to tell her story anonymously was well known in her midwestern community but had been a member of the church she attended for only a couple of years. Although relatively new to that church, she was involved in several groups, including a care group of twelve people. Then she had the sad task of being in charge of the funeral for one of the four members of her immediate family. Although the minister was personally very supportive to the family, it was summer vacation time and no one was in charge of reaching out to bereaved families. What was troubling to her was the absence of any response from church members. No member sent a card, made a visit, or sent food. In the course of the next thirteen months, this woman buried two more of her immediate family. Again, none of the members of this church acknowledged the pain that was felt in this home. The woman began to entertain thoughts of suicide and left the church. To my knowledge, no one ever asked why.

I found this story shocking, because it had been my experience during my childhood in Texas that when illness or death occurred, church members, friends, neighbors, and even strangers came in a constant stream, offering concern and carrying flowers and every conceivable kind of food. I have been told that in the upper midwestern region of our country, people are afraid that going to a home or calling will be perceived as intrusive.

Contrast this woman's experience with a church that was its polar opposite but was located in the same geographical area. Sometime after Martha's disappearance, a friend invited me to visit her church. I arrived before my friend and waited for her at the entrance. As soon as the usher spotted me standing by the door, he began introducing me to others members, telling me a bit about each person as he introduced them to me. After several introductions, I was not left alone to await my friend or find a seat on my own. I was asked to join the people who had been talking to me. They told me, "We will save a place for your friend." After the service, I left feeling wonderful, but that was only the beginning.

That evening, about suppertime, my doorbell rang. When I answered, there stood a man and woman whom I had never seen before. They told me they lived in the neighborhood and were members of the church I had visited. They didn't want to come in; they just wanted to let me know they were glad I had come, hoped I would come back, and told me they had brought me an apple pie for my supper. They went even further and offered to be of service to me. They knew I lived alone, so the man told me he had several teenage sons, and if I needed any chores done, he would bring them by and do them for me. I did go back to that church, and each time I saw the couple, the man repeated the offer.

On the fourth offer, I told him there was something, but it was so small I hesitated to ask him to make a trip for it. I had a very heavy chair in the living room that was in the wrong location, so I asked if they would move it for me. No problem! One afternoon the following week, he came by with one of his sons. They moved the chair in about thirty seconds then joined me for a cup of tea and a short chat. (I later learned that when you join that church you are given a small white towel to symbolize the towel Jesus used to wash the feet of the disciples. This was meant to remind you that as a member you served one another.) Members of that church did all sorts of things for each other, large and small. If you needed the roof replaced on your home, a group of men arrived to do it. Later in the day, women would bring food for the workers. I imagined it was similar to an old-fashioned barn raising.

From time to time, members held neighborhood dinners. The church membership was divided into neighborhoods, with one family in each who would organize a dinner in the home of a church member who lived in that area so we could get to know each other. I was often pleasantly surprised when people invited me to come home with them after church to have dinner with their family. After joining that church, I was never alone again for a holiday meal. One young woman who could not be with her own mother on Mother's Day "adopted" me as her mom for the holiday and took me out to lunch.

Sunday had always been my favorite day of the week. I loved going to church with friends to worship God. The glow of morning worship spilled over into the afternoon and evening hours. But after Martha's death and after Kay enrolled in the University of Georgia, I began to spend my Sundays alone. Then Sunday afternoon and evening seemed to drag on forever. This church saved me from the danger that my aloneness could have produced.

In addition to emotional, spiritual, and physical well-being, our very survival can depend on our connectedness. When talking about this subject with Brad Mitchell, my minister at Trinity Church, he reminded me of a segment often shown on PBS's *The Wild Kingdom*. The scene opens with the camera focused on a majestic, powerful lion surveying the landscape in search of prey. Spotting a herd of Thomson's Gazelles or wildebeests, the lion begins to stalk. As the chase ensues, the mighty lion separates one animal from the pack— one that is slower, younger, or weaker—before going in for the kill. Once alone, the poor creature is doomed, but those who stay grouped together are safe. This is a fitting parable for the human condition.

Unlike animals, whose instinct tell them not to travel alone, humans often develop pride in being self-sufficient and invite disaster by their determination to remain separate from those who could strengthen them. We often hesitate to reach out for help for fear that we will be a burden to others and use up our quota of favors. In American culture, we have somehow come to value independence and rugged individualism to the detriment of all. We often fail to appreciate the civilizing influence of being loved by others and fail to recognize that separateness can be just as deadly a risk to individuals and society as it is to the animal separated from its pack. We do, of course, have an advantage as humans, because we have the capacity to see the danger when someone strays into perilous territory and can seek to shepherd them back into safety if we recognize what is happening.

Prior to developing this insight, I felt guilty, even selfish, about my need for friends. I find it strange that I never considered fellowship that important in God's scheme of things. Sure, it felt wonderful, but I thought things like prayer were infinitely more importance to our creator. It amazes me now how long it took me to realize that fellowship is more than a wonderful feeling; it is a biblical imperative. Fellowship, after all, was God's very purpose for creating humankind. And I am brought back to the fact that Jesus himself modeled it for us by selecting twelve men with whom to share his life.

Many will agree that tragedy is somehow lessened and joy enhanced by the presence of good friends. I know that without the immediate support of my friends Gerry Shaver, Laurie Downes, and Grace Bowes, I don't think I could have stood it when Martha disappeared. And despite the miles that separated us, Mary Kay and I were united by the fellowship of suffering, first in 1977 when she learned of Martha's disappearance, then in 1980 when her beloved husband Mel died and I lost both of my parents, and again when Mary Kay's daughter died. My respect and love for her increased as a result of the caring attitude she showed to me. She never acted as if sharing my pain was a burden to her. On the contrary, it was a vital part of what her life was all about.

Just as Jesus promised, the fellowship of two or three upholds and encourages faith. It enriches, strengthens, invigorates, and energizes. It increases hope. In times of celebration, it intensifies joy; in seasons of despair, it mitigates pain. And just as he promised, the Lord himself is with us, in some profoundly unique way that I cannot understand, whenever two or three are gathered in his name.

10 The Dawn Will Come

In 1980, eleven months following the memorial service for Martha, my father died. Six weeks later, my mother died. And around that same time, Mary Kay's beloved husband, Mel, died. When Mel married Mary Kay, he enthusiastically adopted all of the consultants as "his daughters." He was as kind and encouraging as his wife was, and we all loved him. As he was dying, he was aware that the date of a company conference where Mary Kay was scheduled to appear was fast approaching. He urged her to make plans to go, but she told him she chose to stay with him instead. On the first day of the week that the conference was scheduled, Mel died. After the memorial service, Mary Kay honored Mel's wishes, and last-minute arrangements were made to fly her to the conference. When she stood on the stage before us and told us that this was the place that Mel had wanted her to be, there was not a dry eye in the vast audience.

She had comforted me, and I wanted to find some way to reach out to her. Then I thought of something I had read that had been helpful to me when Martha vanished. I bought a copy of *Life after Life* by Raymond Moody, a book that describes true experiences of life after death, and sent it to Mary Kay. On July 17 she wrote:

Dearest Sue,

Your precious letter and the book, Life after Life, *has just arrived. It is amazing how many times that things happen all at once. The other night at the American Academy of Achievement Awards, I sat next to Elisabeth Kübler-Ross, who did the foreword to this book. She has promised to send me the three books that she has written, and I have never talked to a more fascinating person. I am taking the book along with me to read on the way to the Los Angeles Jamboree. I can't wait. You are so sweet to share it with me.... I think of you so often, and I know the trials and tribulations you have endured, but you have only become stronger because of them—and I will too. Thank you for caring. Looking forward to seeing you,*

> *Love you,*
> *Mary Kay*

In the eighties, I was aware that the clock was ticking toward a release date for Don Miller, the serial killer who had murdered my daughter. But there seemed to be nothing productive that I could do about it, so during the next eight years I focused as little as possible on the likelihood of Don's release. Since the idea of uprooting my life and leaving my home, my friends, my church, and my business in Michigan and relocating in some new area was a sad prospect, I tried to live one year at a time. During the months surrounding the annual parole hearing, my attention was caught up in speculation. I was thankful for the wide community support at the parole hearings and the enduring friendships I formed there. I could count on the dynamic presence of Jeff Sauter, the Eaton County prosecutor, Donna Irish, the stepmother of two of the victims, and representatives from the East Lansing police department. All of these friends took the fight very, very personally. We never received feedback from the parole board during the hearing, so it was always unsettling to wait for weeks to see whether we had been successful in making our case and wonder how many years we could continue to make the case against his release.

My business also began to flourish in the eighties. I won my first car in 1980, a pink Buick, and in 1981 I started driving the Pink Cadillac in recognition of the achievements of our unit. I sent Mary Kay a copy of an article that appeared in the local paper. The reporter wanted a picture of me and my "pink trophy on wheels," and she was very specific about the type of picture. The reporter wanted me on top of the hood of the Cadillac. So, dressed in my director's suit and high heels, I dutifully climbed on top. The weather that day wasn't the best. As a light rain came down, I reclined across the hood of the car while the pictures were quickly snapped. I was surprised that the focus of the piece was more about my "starting a new life" than about my Mary Kay business, and I was shocked that the picture turned out so well that no one could tell that it had been raining. This is what I heard from Mary Kay:

> *You have indeed made good news. WHAT A WONDERFUL STORY!!! Yes, perhaps God did have something a little different in mind for your story—not so much the company, but what a great Director we have in your vicinity! He does work in mysterious ways His miracles to perform. Not only can you be of tremendous assistance to the people in your unit, but perhaps others will find strength from your courage.*

When the first consultant car program was instituted, Susie Moore was among the first to complete her qualifications to win a free car. Susie continued to win cars, first as a consultant and then as a director. She broke the belief barrier for those in our unit, so other consultants followed her.

Since I had faced such significant life-and-death problems, I was always astonished at the tiny problems that seemed to stop some people. I have great sympathy for those truly in trouble, but I find it hard to deal with someone who makes a tragedy out of a stubbed toe. In order to inspire those who faltered and honor those who were extraordinary, I instituted The Young Wonder's Medal of Valor Program. Our motto, taken from Isaiah, became, "They shall mount up with wings as eagles." Recipients of the award were honored for truly exceptional acts, such as continuing to run a flourishing business while a husband was battling a life-threatening illness, doing profitable Christmas sales in the middle of winter ice storms in Montana, or finishing up the year as Queen of Sales with a broken arm. When I challenged my consultants to do certain things, I would sometimes report to Mary Kay what each consultant had done, and Mary Kay would write each a personal letter of congratulations. I always found it truly extraordinary that she not only wrote all these inspiring individual letters but also acted as if she was delighted to do so.

Life was exciting again. We had unit members winning cars and appearing in the Queen's Court of Sales at the seminar. I was again writing Mary Kay about my ideas for my business. In one letter, Mary Kay commented on a couple of my ideas that I was implementing.

> *Your suggestion, regarding marketing men's products, is most intriguing, and I love your ideas. I am passing that part of your letter on to Dick Bartlett.... It is true we have virtually ignored the Mr. K line, and I agree with you it's time we did something about it.*
>
> *I love your Five-Year Plan that you have developed. It is certainly something that would give long-range planning to new Consultants so that they would not be discouraged before they even get started.*

In the midst of all the positive things that were happening, there was the occasional nagging thought: "What do I do when I know Don Miller is being released?" So I discussed it with Mary Kay via mail, wondering if my name could disappear from the roles of the company and be replaced by a brand new name and identity. Perhaps, I wondered, I could move to a new area and safely list myself in the yellow pages under that new name. Mary Kay replied,

> *I have just received your most thought-provoking letter and I am passing the part about Don Miller on to Monty Barber as he is better qualified to suggest what you can do.... I can certainly understand how you would be afraid if he was paroled.*

I didn't realize at the time that I would soon be facing a different kind of killer, a silent one.

11 Through the Valley of the Shadow

Because of Mary Kay's crusade against breast cancer, we had been introduced to Dr. Amanullah Khan, an oncologist. For several years, Dr. Khan joined Mary Kay on stage at the seminar to raise awareness about breast cancer. When Rena Tarbet, our Company Queen of Sales, became desperately ill with a breast cancer that had spread to other organs, Mary Kay insisted that she go to see Dr. Khan. After Dr. Kahn became Rena's doctor, he was instrumental in miraculously rescuing her from the brink of death and sending her cancer into complete remission. Because of this, I decided that if ever I contracted cancer, I would go to Dallas to see Dr. Khan.

In 1988, three days after I received the bad news that I had cancer, I was in Dr. Khan's office. Following surgery for colon cancer, my daughter Kay and my friend Myrtie, whom I had "adopted" as my sister, were waiting for me in my room. Shortly after I opened my eyes, Mary Kay walked into the hospital room with my doctor in tow. She had Dr. Khan hold the flowering plant she had brought, while she carried a lovely white basket filled to overflowing with candy kisses topped with an enormous bouquet of balloons attached to the handle. On the card Mary Kay had written:

To my beloved friend, Sue.
Hang in there!
Love,
Mary Kay

She clutched a book under her arm, *Survivors Living with Cancer.* I remember that I was still so sleepy that I could manage only one sentence, which was to apologize for not being able to carry on a conversation. Of course, Mary Kay had not expected me to be able to talk to her, so she did the talking. She knew I was alert enough to listen, so she related things that would interest me and chatted with Kay and Myrtie.

It so happened that the day of my surgery, May 12, was Mary Kay's birthday. The staff at the corporate offices had held a birthday luncheon for her. During her visit she related the details of the luncheon, including the fact that they had served her favorite Mexican food. As busy as the day was, and with packing still to do for her trip, here she was at the hospital, visiting me. She wanted to assess with her own eyes how things were going. Before she left, she wrote down her phone number and handed it to Kay. She wanted Kay to call her daily with a report. The year 1988 had brought health challenges to both of us. While I battled cancer, Mary Kay had knee surgery. After her time under the knife and the painful aftermath, she joked, "The doctor forgot to put in the WD-40."

By the time my lab reports from the surgery came and my doctor announced the findings, Mary Kay had left Dallas and was on her way to her meeting with fellow recipients of the Horatio Alger Award. Perhaps she had suspected what I would be facing when she brought me the book *Survivors Living with Cancer*, and perhaps she even knew that I would need the book more than I realized.

Before learning of the test results from Dr. Khan, I was at peace. Believing that the cancer was removed, I thought my task was simply to concentrate on healing from my surgery. So, my body might have been in pain prior to learning of the results, but I was calm and my spirit was light. Emotionally I was okay when Mary Kay visited me, because I thought my only job was to heal.

A couple of days later, however, when my daughter came back into my hospital room, trying to hide the fact that she had been crying, I began to suspect something was terribly wrong. Then Dr. Khan appeared. He brought grim news about the severity of the cancer. Following his visit, I thought, "It's over. This is it! So this is the way my life will end." Fear, panic, despair, and hopelessness flooded over me as I listened to my doctor give the statistical chances for my survival. The specifics were so grim that I just accepted it as fact that this was it, that my life was finished.

The devastating news left me hopeless about surviving. That is when Myrtie and my daughter Kay took over. Their faith was strong and solid. This daughter, who had had her faith in God severely, threatened when her sister was murdered, now spoke words of faith. I don't remember the words Myrtie and Kay spoke, but it was enough to ignite hope. Their faith that God would enable me to beat cancer gradually took over. I began to share that deep assurance that I would live!

The thought came to me that maybe sometimes God allows us to choose whether to give up and die or to fight and live. I chose life! I decided to fight and to live each day. "After all, I am alive today," I reasoned. "After all, each day in this incredible universe is a marvelous gift. There is so much loveliness in people and beauty lavished even in the depths of the sea and forests where no human eye will ever see it. And what a gift it is to be able to experience love and receive love in return. What an awesome and beautiful place we were given to inhabit. What do I have to lose by living in faith? If I spend my days fearfully focused on the disease and filled with anxiety and I die, then I will have wasted the good days in this incredible place; and if I survive, I will still have needlessly thrown away those days."

On Memorial Day, about a week following my release from the hospital, I received an unexpected phone visit from Mary Kay. It was a wonderful, long, leisurely talk. Our conversation covered the gamut, from girl talk and our individual health challenges to reports on the people she had met at the Horatio Alger meeting and her subsequent visit to Hershey Farms. She was very impressed with the orphanage she visited there. "The founders," she told me, "were Milton and Catherine Hershey, who were unable to have children of their own. The Hersheys decided to give homes to orphans. So they built a series of individual cottages to be home for ten to twelve orphans. Each home functioned as a family unit with children of various ages living together. Each had live-in 'house parents.' Dinner was eaten as a family. There were chores to be done, and the 'parents' supervised schoolwork. I am inspired by the solid values and responsible citizens that graduate from these homes."

That visit, she said, gave her a dream of starting an orphanage in the Dallas area. Always the innovator, she was enthused about adding an additional exciting ingredient to her purposed orphanage—a retirement community for Mary Kay directors.

Mary Kay knew that her directors possessed a vast reservoir of wisdom and exciting skills to enrich the lives of children. She also knew that after a lifetime of purpose-driven living, retirement was a concept that had no personal appeal. Many of the national sales directors also resisted the idea of retirement. This plan would allow directors to maintain their camaraderie and sense of purpose even in retirement. The enthusiastic way that Mary Kay talked about her new project left me with the feeling that she herself wanted to be a part of such a community.

The conversation then shifted. Since Mary Kay had just celebrated her birthday, we talked about an idea she had as a result of receiving ten thousand birthday cards. While she appreciated the outpouring of love that those cards represented, they piqued her practical, frugal side. All those beautiful cards, she lamented, had to be thrown away after she opened them. In order to keep them, she would have needed to build an extra room!

"And do you know, Sue," she said with a note of incredulity in her voice, "some cost as much as ten dollars for *one* card! So I started thinking, wouldn't it be wonderful if everyone who wanted to send me a card would instead donate the price of a card to the fight against cancer? Will you help me spread the word among the other directors?" I did as she requested, and the following year our unit eliminated the cards. Instead we sent one letter with our best wishes for her birthday and a check from the ladies in the unit tucked inside.

When our conversation got around to the upcoming annual seminar, I think she intended to encourage me and inspire me with a short-term goal to be well enough to join my Mary Kay family for at least a part of seminar. Even though Mary Kay was going through knee replacement surgery, she was, as usual, unstoppable. In spite of the fact that she couldn't walk around the North Park Mall, she had gone with her childhood friend and ridden on one of the scooters the mall provided. From the way she talked, she seemed to have relished zipping around in her quest for the perfect earrings to go with her ball gown. The mode of Mary Kay's dramatic entrance into seminar each year was always a closely guarded secret. But this year she chose to tell me all about it. She drew me a verbal picture of the fabric and design of her ball gown, complete with descriptions of her accessories. "Sue," she said, "I feel it is important for you to be at the seminar this year, surrounded by your Mary Kay family, even if you are there only for a few sessions."

Though I had a Pink Cadillac in my garage at home, I had no car in Dallas. So in order to make it possible for me to attend the seminar, the company loaned me a Grand Am to park right outside the door of my room at the Marriott. That way I could go back and forth at my own pace.

While in the hospital, I made a decision to be thankful. When it was first suggested that I find things each day to be grateful for, I felt, "Why should I be thankful? What do I have to be thankful for? I am in pain and I might die." But then I began to ponder my situation and to ask myself, "What do I have left?" A funny absurdity popped into my brain. "My hair … I still have some of my hair left." I was thankful for that. That led me to think of other things to be grateful for. I remembered my mother, who was legally blind for the last seventeen years of her life. I watched as the glaucoma first narrowed her vision until all peripheral vision was gone and she saw the world as if she were viewing it through the barrel of a shotgun. Then Mother said it was like a veil fell over what remained, and all that was left was the ability to distinguish between light and darkness. If she had been able to regain her sight for one day, it would have been the happiest day of her life. I had my eyesight. I thanked God for my eyes.

After I made the decision to live, I made another choice. I decided never to repeat the words spoken to me by Dr. Kahn, and I never have. I had been taught the power of the spoken word (which is talked about in many places in the Bible, including the book of James). Once I had experienced this "deep knowing" in my spirit, I knew I would be fine, so I started telling the truth in advance. To those who called, I said, "I am doing fine." I might have carried that a bit to the extreme, however, because one day Myrtie had had enough. She had just watched me sit at the table for an hour trying to eat a bowl of chicken soup with a piece of baked potato mashed up in it. Because my mouth and throat were so filled with sores, swallowing was painful. When I received a call from a friend whose opening question was, "How are you?" and I had made my habitual response, "Great!" gracious, soft-spoken Myrtie grabbed the phone from my hand and announced, "When Sue says she's feeling great, she is feeling like hell!" Then she proceeded to tell the caller what was happening. After that, I realized Myrtie needed to know if I was better or worse than the day before.

I made additional decisions to cooperate in my own healing. I decided to rejoice and be glad in each new day, regardless of the physical reality. I also became determined to fight the cancer on all fronts, starting with prayer, because all healing comes from God. Then I would fight the cancer with medical help and follow the diet that was prescribed for me; and I would exercise. I was determined to fight with body, mind, soul, and spirit. I listened to praise songs and healing passages of scripture on a cassette player with a pillow speaker that my friend Betty brought to me. Music is powerful because it bypasses the conscious brain and goes directly to the spirit. And the words of the Bible spoke with authoritative power to my heart; they brought comfort, strength, and peace like no other words could.

I continued to find things each day to be grateful for: great friends who encouraged me, business associates who stood by me, and a beautiful daughter full of faith; I was thankful for eyes to see and also legs and arms that worked, and, yes, even for having enough hair to fit on four rollers when I washed it and for Myrtie, who, like a sister, took me in between hospital stays so that I would not have to face my illness alone. This wonderful servant-hearted woman even learned to cook only what I was allowed to eat on my limited diet.

I also moved part of my office into my hospital room during the monthly chemo sessions. That way I could continue to help my consultants. I decided not to dwell so much on my illness that I failed to see the needs of others. I reached out with words of encouragement to the hospital staff, for they could be hurting also. All of them perform essential services, even those who wash the floors and clean the rooms and hallways. Without them, infection would become a killer, but how often are they made to feel how important their work is? This thinking was a direct result of the influence Mary Kay had on me. Before meeting her, I took a lot of things for granted without taking the time to say thank you.

I had read of Norman Cousins' laugh therapy. When Cousins developed a life-threatening illness and standard medicine was not helping, he decided to test his theory that laughter is healing. He checked himself out of the hospital and checked into a hotel where he could have a private nurse and could rest undisturbed. His treatment consisted of massive doses of vitamin C and viewing funny movies. He found that periods of hearty laughter produced long intervals where he was free of pain. By following this regimen, he was completely healed. The ancient wisdom of the Bible speaks of a merry heart doing good, like a medicine, so I resolved to laugh some each day. Kay arranged for her father to bring a TV and video player into my room. Each of the six weeks I was in the hospital, he willingly brought in a stack of funny videos twice a week, even though we had been divorced for years.

Mary Kay's knee surgeries were also painful, and I wanted Mary Kay to experience pain relief. Since my friends were sending me funny cards and articles, I passed on some of the funniest ones to Mary Kay. One of the things I sent her was a humorous article about the strange things that occur in air travel. I thought Mary Kay would particularly relate to that, because she was used to spending long hours on planes. Another was a definition of hospital terms for the layman. "Barium," for example, was defined as "what you do when a patient dies," and "outpatient" is a person who has fainted. I also recommended especially good videos to help in her recovery. She replied,

> *We know that laughter is the best medicine, and the article you sent from the* Chicago Tribune *was a hoot! That one should be used in the next* Airplane *sequel. Thanks for the laugh—and also thanks for the video recommendation. I'll see if we can pick it up.*

Again, <u>thank you</u> for sharing. Your caring and friendship mean so very much to me during this time.

Chemotherapy—I dreaded going through that more than anything else. I simply could not imagine how I would survive it. The cancer center only had private rooms, so I pictured myself lying in a small room by myself, sick as a dog for five long days and nights. Since I had a month following surgery before my body would be healthy enough to start chemo, the anxiety had a very long time to build. Myrtie is a woman of prayer, so we became prayer partners. We prayed about everything. As we were praying about the upcoming chemo, she suggested that instead of dreading chemo, I should welcome it as a friend. One day, as I was undergoing one of many tests, I was hooked up to a clear liquid drip going into my vein. It looked exactly like the chemo would look, and yet I was fine. The fluid was not making me nauseated, so I did as Myrtie suggested, and my fear was gone.

The day came for the first round of chemo. Myrtie was sitting there with me as I lay in the hospital bed. We went on chatting and paying no attention to the process of starting the chemo drip. The task was finished, and Myrtie kept visiting until she could see that I was doing fine. Then she left. My first visible miracle was this: no nausea, ever! In fact, I had the opposite reaction. I ate like a horse. I had not been overweight before surgery, but in the month following, I had lost about seventeen pounds. While chemo was dripping into my veins, I ate everything on my tray, even things I ordinarily would not eat. In between, I ate snacks of yogurt with fruit. I liked fish, but not fish that smells really fishy. Ordinarily, the stinky fish that I was served would have made me sick to my stomach. Not this fish! I managed to eat it by turning my tray around and pushing it as far away from my nose as I could reach. I ate every morsel. They could not fill me up! I had the appetite of an adolescent male. Somehow the nurses had neglected to offer me any medication for nausea. On my fifth chemo treatment, I was offered it for the first time, and my response was, "No! Don't even mention it."

I feel I had been prepared for my battle against cancer in several ways. I had now spent years changing from disaster thinking to positive thinking in building my Mary Kay business. The image that now came to me was that God was sending electrical charges roaming through my body, zapping any lingering cancer cells with tiny bursts of light and destroying them.

Another blessing was that I didn't have to worry about being fired for taking too much sick leave. My income was dependable. In fact, it actually increased. Mary Kay told me, "Sue, don't worry about a thing; just concentrate on getting well." This was possible, because by this time in my career I had built a solid foundation. I had trained women from my unit who had become directors, so the company paid me a monthly commission on their volume. Plus, I had an established, well-trained group of consultants who had goals of their own, and I was paid a commission on their sales from the corporate pocket. National sales director Sherrill Steinman reached out with help and "adopted" my people while I was absent from Michigan. She invited them to attend her sales meetings and to contact her for any assistance that they needed while I was gone. My consultants and directors didn't stop working or reaching for their goals because I was ill, so my monthly income was dependable. I was so thankful that I was not in the position of a lady I knew whose sick leave was used up and who had to go to work, even when she felt sick as a dog, in order to keep her job and to keep her monthly check coming in. On the other hand, my consultants and directors were not going to stop building their businesses simply because I was sick. In fact, my consultants and directors did so well in my absence from Michigan, where the majority of my associates live, that my income increased by ten thousand dollars that year.

In a handwritten note, Mary Kay responded to one of my letters:

Dearest Sue,

Your letter was a BRIGHT spot in my day! How wonderful that your fantastic unit "hung in there!" even with you gone and earned your Cadillac. What a <u>great</u> <u>group</u>! Give them a hug for me.

I know that the next few months will be difficult with the chemo, interferon, etc.—but you've already SHOWN you are an IRON lady!

A constant theme of Mary Kay's letters during this period was,

"Please take care of yourself and do all the things you are supposed to. We want you back healthy and well!" I assured her that I would. Not only did Mary Kay write encouraging notes and letters to me, she also sent a beautiful letter to Myrtie to thank her for taking care of me.

In November 1988, Mary Kay shared her good news with me:

> *I have been able to feel your love and prayers—and they are working! The doctor feels that I am ahead of schedule in my recovery, but of course, it will take time for my "bionic knees" to be fully functional, so keep praying!*

Shortly before Christmas the following year, I shared good news with Mary Kay, and she penned these words:

> *My heart is leaping with JOY at your wonderful news— No more tests!!!!!! <u>Clear</u> of cancer—WOW! God does answer prayers!*
>
> *It is indeed a miracle, and I am simply elated. I could not have asked for a more wonderful Christmas present. We have all worried because we knew it was serious. To have this news makes Christmas complete.'*

Before I had cancer, I had always felt that if I ever did get the disease, I would live thereafter in a constant state of fear, worried that it would return. While there were times when threats arose, they proved to have no substance. Because God has been so gracious to me, that kind of fear did not arise. Instead, I have lived in a state of "knowing" that the cancer is gone. Occasionally people have said, "Oh, you are in remission." My instant response is, "No, it is gone. God healed me." The road was not easy, and there were times when I lived with anxiety, but the experience left me high on life, with a profound sense of awe and gratitude to God. Soon after the cancer was diagnosed, I was with a young woman who was the associate pastor of my church (this young pastor's physical appearance and her passion reminded me of Martha). We had been praying in the somber, cathedral-like sanctuary when she said to me, "You will come back here and shout, 'Yay, God!' because you will be well." At the time, I was not quite sure about such an expression. I had the feeling that it would not be respectful. However, after I was healed, I remembered her words, and now the expression seemed totally appropriate. In the years since, I have declared "Yay, God!" many times. After coming through this experience, life is somehow richer, sweeter. I started a daily practice of searching for spots of beauty tucked away in hidden places. I live with heightened senses; colors are brighter, and my daughter Kay and my friends are dearer.

About nine months after the surgery, I had another colonoscopy. The doctor found one small but benign polyp. When I told Kay, she said, "Mother, I don't know whether to tell you this or not, but after your surgery, the surgeon told me that if he had been able to prepare you, he would have taken the entire colon instead of just the third that he took, because your colon was just loaded with hundreds and hundreds of polyps!" Praise God, he didn't need to. Through the years there have been other polyps removed, and there have been a few scary times. On May 12, 2008 it was twenty years since he healed me.

I believe it is no coincidence that again, at the very time I was writing this chapter, a shadow again tried to engulf me. On May 1, 2007, I had what I assumed was another routine colonoscopy. I awakened to learn there was a polyp that was too large to be removed and that a biopsy had been taken. I immediately turned to my prayer partners to ask for prayer. In spite of the good news that the polyp was not malignant, I was a bit down. They were talking about performing major surgery to remove it. Both the surgeon in Lansing and the surgeon I saw later in San Diego said that the polyp was so large, there was a good likelihood that they would find cancer cells somewhere in the tissue. Ugh! Because there was probably scar tissue from my previous colon surgery, I was not a good candidate for a small incision. To say I didn't want to go through that again was quite an understatement. I was not looking forward to surgery or the recovery time afterward. The good news was that the polyp was located in the lowest part of the colon, the sigmoid colon.

I wish I could say that I approached this circumstance in my life with great faith and with the peace of God, but I didn't. Because of all the tasks to be done before surgery, I was not in constant contact with my prayer partners. And I would pay a price for that. I prepared a bit like a Lone Ranger. For some reason, I started sorting my books. During this process I picked up *The Helper* by Catherine Marshall, which is a book about the Holy Spirit. It had been on my bookshelf for years, but I had never read it. It was now going to be a help to me.

When I was doing the unpleasant prep two hours before my appointment with the gastroenterologist in San Diego, I experienced all sorts of difficultly and discomfort. It literally raised my blood pressure. Before the second prep an hour later, I remembered something from Catherine's book that seemed unimportant at the time. When I first read it I remember thinking "Well, I *know* that." The part I had dismissed talked about the need to ask the Holy Spirit's help in everything, no matter how mundane. It occurred to me at that moment that during the first prep I hadn't asked for the Holy Spirit's help. So before I started the second prep, I simply asked for help. And wow, what a difference! It went in fast and easy and flowed well, and I was through in a fraction of the time it had taken me before!

Another thing I had been praying for was favor. That prayer started to be answered immediately. I knew that my surgeon needed my medical records right away so he could decide what tests to order, if any, and get them done before surgery. My experience in the past has been that records are difficult to obtain in a timely manner. The fact that I needed two sets of records from two different states made getting the records quickly twice as difficult. Incredibly, each lady in the respective record department took care of the request immediately. When I found out that my doctor's office received a fax from both places the very day of my request, tears of gratitude started to flow because of the favor I had received.

Afterward, as I went on my routine walk up the hill to absorb the recently discovered benefits of vitamin D from the sun and gain all the strength I could before the operation, I did so with a grateful heart. Because of the thanksgiving in my heart, I was now able to enjoy the delicious cool breeze and the magnificent flowers. I'd experienced them the day before, but they had failed to stir my emotions. Now I was again at peace.

That peace lasted only a short time. In spite of knowing the favor I had just been granted in answer to prayer, the dread of surgery and whatever aftermath it might bring returned to depress me to the point that I felt like I could not endure it. Instead of remaining confident in light of the gift of grace I had just received, I said to God, "I can't stand this! I can't go through another major surgery." In the days prior to surgery, I frequently used one of Mary Kay's most detested words, "can't." Mary Kay would have told me, "Cut out your tongue!" But Mary Kay's words were far from mind. Negative thoughts continued to flow. "I am so tired of fighting. I can't go through cancer again. In fact, I can't even face the terror I am feeling while counting down the days until I am wheeled into surgery!" The closer surgery came, the more I stewed. I guess I had decided that God had already reached his limit on the miracles he would perform in my life. I was consumed with thoughts of my weakness, and I was seriously involved in one gigantic "pity party."

Finally, I realized, once again, that I had to change my focus. The Holy Spirit reminded me of my self-absorption. I was centered on my fears and my situation. With this insight, I acknowledged I had no power to help myself. Instead of being mired down in myself and my fears, I had to direct my attention to the only one who could help me, the one who does hold the power. The words of a song we sang on the previous Sunday spoke to my situation. I made a copy and asked Kay to put it in her purse so that the words would go with me to the hospital and be a reminder to me, lest I fall prey again to fear. The day came, and the attendants came to wheel me into the surgical suite. Wait a minute," I said, while Kay read the words of KateWilkinson's hymn which she wrote in 1925 entitled "May the Mind of Christ my Savior."

> *May the peace of God my Father rule my life in everything …*
> *May the love of Jesus fill me as the waters fill the sea …*

Good news awaited me as I awakened in the recovery room. My kind colorectal surgeon, Dr. Worsey, told me that he had been able to do laparoscopic surgery instead of "opening me up." Yay! There had been no scar tissue from the previous cancer surgery that blocked his view. (This cut down on pain and time to heal.) However, based on my previous history, my body tended to form scar tissue quickly, particularly in my eyes, resulting in the need for many eye surgeries. So this was a big gift from God—a miracle and not my normal bodily response.

On the second day, more of God's favor was revealed. Dr. Worsey came in and gave me more great news: no cancer cells were anywhere in the tissue! This was the most important news of all.

Good news just kept coming. On the third day I was told that the polyp was much smaller than it had appeared because it was sitting on a bed of diverticulitis. I had been having trouble for months with my digestive track; and amazingly, all the problem areas were concentrated along ten inches where the polyp was, so he just removed all of that. (What are the chances of all the problems being confined to one area?) That meant in time I would be able to eat salads, seeds, nuts, raw fruits, and vegetables. Wow! What a gift! And he also said I might not need any more colonoscopies, because my colon is now so short that he may be able to see it all in the office. That would be huge also.

Following Dr. Worsey's visit on the second day, and in spite of my lack of faith in the weeks before surgery, God began lavishing me with the undeserved gifts of gratitude and praise. It was not an act of obedience that I responded with praise; it just welled up inside me and became as much a part of me as breathing. I just began basking in his favor. And even in the intense pain and the mundane hospital routine, the melody and words to the song "Give thanks with a grateful heart" ran continuously in my head. I never tired of the glorious beauty of the music. Not only in the conscious daytime hours, but even throughout the night, as I aroused from sleep, that song replayed in my consciousness. The pain or the medication didn't touch or dull the music. The words *"give thanks to the Holy One who has given Jesus Christ his Son"* were penned by songwriter Henry Smith; however, the words that I heard to the opening line of his tune were *not* written by him. They were, *"Now let the lame say, I am healed, the sick say I am whole, and the blind say, I see."* I was told these words were not part of Henry Smith's lyrics. In fact, the words that I heard had never been written. However, the lyrics I heard spoke perfectly to my condition: lame because I walk with a cane, sick because I need healing, and blind because I have trouble with my eyesight. I have since concluded that the words I heard must have been the words I needed to hear and were meant for my ears only.

Kay's prayer at our first meal the night she brought me home from the hospital was simply, "*Thank you God for your mercy.*" This spontaneous one-sentence heartfelt prayer pretty well summed it up for the two of us. We both have been and are overwhelmed with the mercy God had directed toward us.

Through it all, my sweet daughter was incredibly kind and attentive while carrying on her demanding full time job. She lovingly did countless things for my safety and to provide as much comfort as possible. She handled it all with good humor and grace. We even found some things to laugh at. I am so blessed to have such a beautiful, loving daughter.

Once again the dark period proved to be only the shadow of death, and the reality is that God healed me yet another time. God has not come to the end of his miracles on my behalf. I am so grateful for the privilege of seeing and experiencing God at work in my life. It is an awesome and exciting way to live.

12 One More Parallel before the Curtain Begins to Fall

Three years after my bout with cancer, Mary Kay and I came to share another tragic experience. In 1991, Mary Kay's only daughter, Marilyn, died. Since Mary Kay had gotten as many as ten thousand cards on a single birthday, I could not imagine how many she would receive after her daughter's death. But I wanted to let her know that I cared. I knew that Mary Kay enjoyed poetry and liked the work of Helen Steiner Rice. I found an appropriate poem written by her and wrote Mary Kay a simple note. Although she must have received an avalanche of mail, I was amazed that she took the time to respond to my simple card with a handwritten note.

> *Dearest Sue,*
>
> *Your precious note was so appreciated. You are one of the few who can really understand how it feels to lose a daughter.*
> *The poem you sent was so meaningful. Thank you. I am so blessed to have friends like you. God bless you!*

Five years later, the final curtain began to fall as Mary Kay entered the final difficult phase of her life. Because of a stroke, she was no longer able to communicate with me. For the first time, a letter I wrote to her was answered by her assistant. I was sad that the stroke had silenced her warm engaging voice, a voice that had profoundly inspired millions. It also ended moments I cherished. Somehow, in a way that I cannot explain, Mary Kay was able to connect simply by returning the gaze of someone across the room, and she was able to connect on a powerful emotional level. I witnessed such an event at a Red Jacket awards luncheon as I sat beside my consultant Colleen. The luncheon was designed to honor consultants who had at least three members on their team.

While waiting for the luncheon to begin, Colleen gazed fondly at Mary Kay, who was seated at the head table. Mary Kay turned and caught Colleen's eye, smiled, and gave her a wink. For a moment, Colleen sat transfixed. Then she turned to me with an incredulous look and said, "She winked at me!" Then she added, "Sue, when Mary Kay looked directly into my eyes, it was as if time stood still and there was no one else in the room except Mary Kay and me. It was so special." Colleen has cherished that memory for almost two decades.

From 1981 until the late 1990s, I had done my best to live my life without looking forward to the time when my daughter's killer would be released from prison. Because I knew he held me responsible for his incarceration, I feared for my life if he were ever released. In early 1997, soon after Mary Kay's stroke, I was given gut-wrenching news by the parole board. In two years, at the age of forty-four, Don Miller would be released and could again walk the streets of East Lansing. Because of quirks in Michigan law at that time, he had completed a reduced minimum sentence and would therefore be released, and he would not be on parole or under police surveillance.

I was never able to share with Mary Kay the high drama and the heroic efforts that transpired after Don Miller's release date had been announced. She would have been pleased to know that I was not alone in this battle. From the beginning, Mary Kay had been able to share my frustrations with Michigan law regarding victims. We had prayed for someone who knew law and would find a way to change it. I wrote an appeal to the local Lansing paper, which is read by Michigan legislators. It appeared on the front page. I also was invited to share my concerns candidly on local TV. All of this, it seemed to me, was of no avail. No one stepped forward. What I did not know, however, was that the seeds to my answer had already been planted in the lives of several prominent people in the area.

One of the key individuals was William VanRegenmorter, who, unbeknownst to me, had been elected in 1982 to the Michigan House after running on a platform to reform crime legislation. He became chair of the House Judicial Committee and later the Senate Judicial Committee. A second key individual was Bonnie Bucquerque, a victim advocate whose life had been personally affected by Don Miller. When Don was due to be released, she refused to accept the proposition that there was no more to be done. The sentencing in Miller's plea bargain had enraged her, and she knew enough about Michigan law to realize that a thirty-year sentence did not mean thirty years served and that he would be released as a young man still capable of pursuing his cruel obsession. Bonnie enlisted the aid of Frank Ochberg, a psychologist known internationally for his work with victims. At Bonnie's urging, Frank began to assemble a team from the community. Frank and those who joined the group became totally dedicated and absolutely determined to find a way to stop Miller from being released, lest he kill again.

I learned of these individuals in 1997 when I was invited to join a group called the Committee for Community Awareness and Protection. Blocking Miller's release seemed impossible, but this group heroically refused to shrug their shoulders and accept that there was nothing they could do. Instead, they worked tirelessly, without pay, and invested their hearts and souls.

Ultimately, by the grace of God, the team of prosecutors led by Jeff Sauter was victorious. And it was on the basis of an idea so ridiculous that a correspondent for *48 Hours* who was filming the trial thought they didn't have a prayer of a chance to convict Miller. I tell the incredible story of how the prosecutors were able to use a shoelace to add an additional sentence for Miller in my book *Lethal Friendship*.

Mary Kay would have been relieved to know that I was no longer engaged in this fight by myself and that community leaders had helped me put a stop to Donald Miller's release.

13 A Victorious Finish for the Most Important American Woman of the Twentieth Century

After her stroke, Mary Kay was seldom in the public eye. I vividly recall that when I first heard of her stroke, my immediate reaction was to think how extremely hard this must be for her. The damage to her speech must have been especially devastating for her, since she was a master communicator who had a wonderfully expressive speaking voice that she used like a finely tuned instrument. Although she was all Texan, her voice carried no hint of a Texas twang; it flowed more like velvet. I had marveled at the youthful sound of her voice. Until the stroke, it had never betrayed her or even hinted at her age. I could only imagine how frustrating it must have been to her to lose her wonderful voice.

Her frustration must have been magnified by the need for a physical therapist. I knew she was not fond of physical therapy. At the time of her knee surgeries, she referred good-naturedly to her physical therapists as "physical torturers," and I knew that following the stroke there must have been new sessions.

Between the time of her stroke and her death, we heard very little news regarding her health. Then, in early November 2001, e-mails started circulating among the directors, which indicated that Mary Kay's health was deteriorating rapidly. Although the source was unofficial, it was the first time e-mails of this type had appeared, so it was troubling news. No additional information came in the weeks that followed. When the first official word came, it gave us the dreaded news that Mary Kay had died on Thanksgiving Day, a holiday that she loved. In all the years that I knew her, gratitude was one of the hallmarks of Mary Kay's life. It seems to me that even the date of her death underscored her belief in the necessity of living a life filled with giving thanks. Although she did not recover physically, her faith and her life principles sustained her during this final period.

Following the memorial service in Dallas, Mary Kay directors began organizing local memorial services to honor her. I was asked to make remarks at the memorial service that the directors of the greater Lansing area planned. As I reflected on Mary Kay's life, my mind was flooded with memories. My church, which had been chosen for the memorial, was decorated for Christmas with huge red poinsettias lining the three steps of the large circular platform at the front of the sanctuary. This provided a magnificent garden setting. I remarked how appropriate it was for Mary Kay's memorial; she would have loved it, for she loved to garden. The home she had built with her husband was built in a circle around an atrium where she could garden, away from the prying eyes of neighbors or tour buses.

As memories surfaced, I was struck by the fact that she never retired from life. All her life, Mary Kay kept dreaming new dreams. Her life testifies to the fact that she was never willing to simply bask in her past achievements. Her vision kept expanding. I recalled our conversation on Memorial Day 1988, when she told me of her dream of starting an orphanage, patterned after the one she had visited in Hershey, Pennsylvania. In the early nineties, I had asked Mary Kay if she still had plans for her orphanage. She said yes but added, "First, the loan from the bank to buy back our stock must be paid back." Her stroke ended that dream.

I thought about the fact that all through her life she had remained a humble woman. Even after years of receiving wild applause just for appearing on stage in front of thousands of consultants, she never considered the applause to be her due. On many of these occasions I watched her standing on stage, smiling at the audience and gently shaking her head as if to say, "What's the big deal here?" Then she would say to her admiring crowd, "Look what *you* have done!" Success didn't change Mary Kay.

Since she gave God the credit for her success, she wasn't impressed with herself. She was never a prima donna. I never saw her throw her weight around or behave in a rude manner to anyone. She was the same person in front of thousands that she was one on one. Her grandson commented on this at her memorial service in Dallas. He told us that when people would ask what his grandmother was like, he told them that she was no different to the public than she was to her friends and family.

I remembered being at a meeting where she was speaking in Detroit and the lights in the ballroom went out in the middle of her speech. Mary Kay paused a moment. Someone brought a candle to the podium. And then, while some of us scrambled to find hotel staff to restore the lights, she calmly resumed with her speech without missing a beat. All the while, she maintained her good humor and would never have dreamed of making the event planner feel badly about the incident. Clearly, people were more important to her than things.

Good memories flooded my mind, memories of people who would never achieve the limelight. Even early on, Mary Kay Inc. was considered a smart career choice for young people with corporate ambitions. She believed a worker on the production line deserved to be treated with the same respect accorded to executives. I watched as the company grew and hired more administrative staff. Mary Kay insisted that every addition to the staff be someone who had a heart for serving others, and she employed a twist in the screening process to ensure this. The company normally brought young applicants to spend a week at the Dallas headquarters. At the end of the week, every person on the staff gave feedback about their experience with the applicant. Mary Kay's maid, the person with the least prestigious job, carried the most weight. If the applicant had been rude to her in any way, the applicant was out of the running.

Mary Kay has been called the most important American woman of the twentieth century. I believe that history will agree with this verdict not only because of the impact she made on American women but also for the global contribution she made to women's lives and to the world of business. Before her death, Mary Kay received a letter from a lady living in China, which is now one of the fastest growing international countries in Mary Kay Inc. The lady wrote that young Chinese consultants were deeply affected by Mary Kay's belief that in order to have a successful life, you put "God first, family second, and career third." As a result, they were going to Christian churches to discover why Mary Kay thought God was so important.

I am so grateful to Richard Rogers, her son, for sharing with all of the directors the video of the magnificent memorial service. As a twenty-year-old man, Richard joined his mother in founding the company. He turned out to be a marketing genius. Before Mary Kay's death, Richard returned to Mary Kay Inc. and assumed the helm of the company.

Richard provided us with a glimpse of how Mary Kay continued to be interested in others. He described how he sat with his mother in her home to watch the annual seminar just a few months before she died. He told us she was thrilled to see the achievements of those who were honored on stage. Other people's success continued to provide her with joy.

The testimonials at her memorial service about the way she lived her last years were awesomely inspiring. They made it abundantly clear that she continued to make a difference in those around her. I think it was very likely that because of her faith in her Lord, this kind of behavior had become so engrained in her personality that she didn't even have to think about it. It has not been an automatic reaction with me; I have had to make a conscious decision, but Mary Kay's response gives me hope that I, too, can come to that point when I no longer have strength.

All of us who loved Mary Kay also owe a debt of gratitude to Charlotte McKinney for the way she ministered to Mary Kay. Charlotte worked for Richard and Mary Kay for twenty-one years. When Mary Kay could no longer go to church, Charlotte asked Richard if she could bring her church to Mary Kay. She started by bringing soloists from St. Andrew United Methodist Church choir to Mary Kay's living room. The church's involvement in ministering to Mary Kay grew until the entire adult choir, as well as the youth choir, came to visit her. Dr. Robert Hasley, St. Andrew's minister, told us that the entire church ultimately adopted Mary Kay. Members stopped by to share devotions and to read the Bible. Although unable to speak, Mary Kay did not stop communicating or enriching others lives. She spoke with her eyes and her hands. She had a profound impact on St. Andrew's minister. He related how tears rolled down her face as she listened to the choir sing "How Great Thou Art" and "Amazing Grace." He said that after the youth choir sang for her, she would not allow them to leave until she had grasped each one's hand and looked deeply into their eyes in thanks. Big strapping football seniors had tears in their eyes as they asked when they could come back to sing for her. When a person read the Bible to Mary Kay, she used her hand to push the Bible back to them to urge them to continue reading. As Dr. Hasley stated, "In my experience, you get to know a person best when they are faced with their most difficult moment. Mary Kay faced her moment with great dignity, class, and deep faith." Through his eyes, we are privileged to see glimpses of the victorious way she lived this final chapter of her life.

Both Dr. Hasley and Dr. Jim Denison, Mary Kay's minister from Park Cities Baptist Church, credited her passionate devotion to the Lord Jesus as the key to her life and legacy. Mary Kay made that commitment to Jesus at the age of seven. "In sharing her faith in a very beautiful way," said Dr. Hasley, "Mary Kay led many people to the Lord, including her husband Mel. It was her faith which enabled her to challenge the existing scripts in order to change this world into a more loving, God-like place."

At last, on that Thanksgiving Day in 2001, the torch was passed to those of us who had captured her vision to enrich the lives of women. I am one who has accepted her challenge to make a difference. Following her lead, I am endeavoring to be a part of continuing to implement her dream through my writing and speaking, particularly in the area of violence in our society.

Postscript

Because of my daughter's murder and the experiences associated with it, a passion now burns in my heart to rein in violence. I have paid an excruciatingly painful price for my education on the subject of violence, knowledge and pain that must not be wasted. We must find a way to end this epidemic of violence. Since Mary Kay's death, the America she loved so very much has grown more violent. We are destroying ourselves from within. Mary Kay would be appalled to learn that 85 percent of the world's serial killers live within the borders of our beloved country. Homegrown terrorists wreak havoc on individuals, schools, workplaces, and communities. Unfortunately, as today's headlines scream of yet another family slaughtered, we pay scant attention.

Perhaps there is a lack of public outrage because we don't realize the magnitude of the problem or because we deny that it can affect us personally or those we love; perhaps it is because we refuse to take responsibility for ourselves or those around us. In her book, *The Death of the Grown-Up*, Diane West, a syndicated columnist with the *Washington Post*, writes that for the first time in the history of the world, a large portion of our citizenry has become adult in years but chosen to remain locked in the self-absorbed, indulgent, irresponsible mindset of adolescence.

Collene Campbell addressed this callousness and lack of outrage when she spoke to a congressional committee in February 2006. She graphically illustrated the scale of the problem when she compared the annual carnage that occurs in the United States to the terrorist attacks on 9/11. She pointed out that every American was justly horrified at the devastation suffered by thousands upon thousands of people. At the same time, she added, we fail to recognize that more than five times as many Americans die each year at the hands of fellow Americans. I had no idea of the magnitude of the problem; the reason we are not aware of this, I suppose, is these Americans die alone, as Martha did, or in small groups, yet in a period of just one year, the total number of violent deaths equals more than five 9/11s! More Americans die violent deaths in nine weeks right here than have died in several years of war in Iraq. This is something the government cannot fix. We, the citizens, will have to make the changes. When we, as communities, decide this is no longer acceptable, we will bring about positive change in our communities.

Mary Kay was not tolerant of wrong. Why are we? If she were here, she would be asking questions, gathering facts. She would take responsibility. She would be about fixing things and not waiting for someone else to do something. When she saw the ravages of breast cancer, she acted.

Although breast cancer and other forms of cancer have not been eradicated from our lives, there has been dramatic progress. Since the days when Mary Kay first brought breast cancer out of the shadows into public discussion, the survival rate has risen dramatically. Today, Mary Kay Inc. through its Mary Kay Ash Charitable Foundation is not alone in being a corporate sponsor in the fight against breast cancer. The Mary Kay practice of donating money from the sale of various products has been adopted by numerous corporations.

The progress in public support for this cause was spotlighted by First Lady Laura Bush, who lit the White House with pink spotlights to support the crusade against breast cancer. Successes in both the breast cancer movement and Mothers Against Drunk Driving encourage me to think that we can have similar success in fighting abuse. MADD has completely changed the paradigm in the way we think about drunkenness. I can remember a time when drunkenness was a joke, when a person could get away with anything if they were intoxicated. Mothers who have had their children killed by drunken drivers changed all that.

There are also signs of hope all over the country in the area of violence. The Mary Kay Ash Charitable Foundation, for example, provides grants to shelters across the nation to help in providing space for women and children. The foundation also provides information and education to help break the silence. The community of High Pointe, North Carolina, is another example of those rays of hope. This town had a neighborhood where it was so violent that the police would not step outside their squad cars. But then a minister, his congregation, and town leaders decided to take back their city. United, they have decreased the violent crime rate 20 percent when it was up 2 percent nationwide, and police officers now walk the streets and mingle with the townspeople who stood up to the thugs. San Diego, California, is yet another example. Thirty-five different agencies working together in the Family Justice Center in San Diego are positively affecting the cycle of violence. Casey Quinn, one of the visionaries who started the center says, "We either reach a child who comes from an abusive home environment before age twelve or we lock them up at age fifteen." For example, one young man who came through the center is now attending college instead of heading for prison.

Liberty can thrive only in a society where the vast majority of the rank and file of its citizenry are committed to being actively responsible members of that community. We need to deal with the breeding grounds that are producing a new generation of self-indulgent cowards and thugs who are creating an unprecedented wave of violence in this country. We need to rein in the "god" of unchecked individual freedom and license. We cannot abandon our streets to rising violence, rape, and murder. We need to start asking questions. I believe Mary Kay would encourage us to ask ourselves not only what are we doing wrong to produce such violence, but what are we willing to change?

Coincidentally, when Mary Kay became physically unable to play an active role in our fight to keep a serial killer from getting out of prison, the battle intensified. In order to generate support for the needed legislation, my Mary Kay family of consultants and directors stepped up to the plate. They joined with me in distributing and collecting petitions all over the state. The petitions advocated civil commitment legislation to prevent the release of serial killers. When I testified on behalf of the passage of this bill, my Mary Kay family packed the Senate Judicial Committee room in support. The bill had bipartisan sponsorship and passed the full Senate unanimously. We also had the votes to pass the bill in the House. However, the chairwoman in the House who received the bill from the Senate would not allow the Senate bill to come to the floor of the House for a vote. As a result of this one person's actions, the bill has not yet been enacted into law. Michigan still needs this law.

Also, when Marc Klaas, a victim advocate and father of Polly Klaas, and I spoke at the international conference on serial killers hosted by the Committee for Community Awareness and Protection, Lansing directors helped to advertise this public event, sell tickets, and usher. Mark's young daughter Polly had been abducted from her bedroom in the middle of the night and died at the hands of her sadistic kidnapper.

We, the millions of individuals who have been touched by Mary Kay's life and legacy plus millions more who believe in peace and justice, now have the power to change our society, just as Mary Kay once did. One life can make a difference. Mary Kay proved that by joining her life with others.

Because of Mary Kay's legacy, her people have been and can again be a force to be reckoned with. May I challenge each of you to become that force? To assist you in thinking about this, I have placed some suggestions in the appendix under the headings: "Haunting Questions," "What Can One Person Do?" "Handling Tragedy," and "Warning Signs."

I know Mary Kay would say we *can* end this epidemic of violence. In her lifetime, Mary Kay was never content to cover the scars of battered women with our wonderful "yellow day radiance concealer." She wanted to do more, and she would also ask us to do more. I can just see her trademark phrase that she often penned at the bottom of her letters:

You can do it!

And I believe she would add: Working together, you can make a difference!

Appendix

Haunting Questions to Discuss and Consider

1. What are we doing wrong to produce such violence?
2. What kind of society do we want for our future and that of our children?
3. Is it a society where every nine weeks as many Americans die at the hands of our fellow countrymen as died in the 9/11 terrorist attack? Is this the country we want for our future?
4. Why is it that 85 percent of the world's serial killers live in America?
5. Are we teaching our young people to become violent?
6. Why do we tolerate bad behavior from public figures such as judges, sports figures, media, elected officials, and business leaders? This behavior will continue as long as we are willing to put up with it.
7. Is there anything we are willing to give up to keep our children safe?
8. Why do we reward celebrities who are terrible role models for our children with large sums of our money for their events? Is amusement more important than character?
9. What do violent video games that teach our citizens to murder have to do with free speech?

10. Why it is legal to provide visual images that teach Americans of any age how to become killers?
11. What are we willing to change to protect our children from abduction and rape?
12. Is pornography a victimless crime? Consider what the feminist Andrea Devorkin asserts: "Pornography is the celebration of rape and injury to women (and children)."
13. Why is there an epidemic of depression among young people here in the most affluent country in the world?
14. Isn't there something wrong with the fact that we have almost three times as many animal shelters as there are shelters for women and children trying to escape abuse?
15. How can we get the media to the table?
16. What role does the media play in our culture of violence? Has the media become the story?
17. How can we get industry leaders to the table to consider the effects of the products they make on the culture of violence?
18. Can we teach compassion?
19. Would there be a benefit to having schools adopt retirement homes?
20. It all boils down to this: What is our vision for the kind of America we want?

During World War II, schoolchildren were trained to seek shelter under their desks in case of an air raid. This was appropriate when schools might be attacked from the air, but does it make sense now when an armed gunman might be roaming the halls? In such a case, might it not be better to follow the example of the passengers on United Airlines Flight 93 and use the things at hand and hurl books, backpacks, chairs, and even pens? Could better protection from a desk be achieved by picking it up for cover to use as a weapon against the attacker? One Lone Ranger is no match for an armed gunman, so isn't it time we started talking about ways to take individual responsibility for helping each other during times of danger?

What Can One Person Do?

1. Slow down. Observe what is going on around you. Ask yourself: How can I make a difference?
2. Replace rude behavior with acts of kindness.
3. Check out what is going on locally where people are making a difference, such as shelters for women and children, violence prevention programs, anger management classes, police auxiliary activities, the Salvation Army, and church organizations.
4. Invite friends, church groups, neighbors, and local Mary Kay consultants and directors to discuss the haunting questions listed and consider what you can do.
5. Take these same questions to the media and to members of local government and parent-teacher associations.
6. Check out the Mary Kay Ash Charitable Foundation Web site at www.mkacf.org.
7. Check out the Family Justice Center Web site at *www. familyjusticecenter.org*. The Family Justice Center opened in San Diego in 2002 and five years later already had twenty-five centers around the United States and ten centers in foreign countries.
8. Go to your local prosecuting attorney or district attorney's Web site.
9. Read the true mystery thriller *Lethal Friendship*. See how local citizens' actions led to the capture of a serial killer when an off-duty fire chief and a worker from a Lansing GM plant stopped to help a rape victim. Later, other citizens of the Lansing area banded together to prevent the same killer from being released into the community. The book may be ordered through the Web site www. lethalfriendship.com.

Handling Tragedy

Whenever someone around you—friend, church member, coworker, or neighbor—is in trouble, show up with something—a rose, a chicken from the deli, but *something*—just to say, "I'm sorry. I care." And don't be tempted to say anything else. Don't criticize or condemn. In the aftermath of tragedy, if someone is angry with God, that's okay. Don't criticize the person for feeling that way, because God didn't appoint you his defense attorney. What he does want is for you to be his loving presence in human form.

1. When trouble comes to you, accept help. Accept it graciously and with appreciation for both small and large acts of kindness. We were not created to be Lone Rangers. From the beginning, God said, "It is not good for man to be alone." In Proverbs we read, "A rope of three strands is not easily broken."
2. Don't focus so completely on your trouble that you fail to see the needs of others. Remember that Jesus, even in his agony on the cross, was thinking of others. He saw his mother and provided for her. He gave life to a dying thief. Focus upward and outward, not inward.
3. Nourish the capacity to feel gratitude and appreciation.
4. Refuse to harbor bitterness. Instead, think about the words in Philippians and concentrate on what is true, lovely, and of good report.
5. God has called us to make a difference, to be salt and light to the world, so get involved in stopping the violence.

Signs of Danger

Some people prefer not to look at this topic because they want to concentrate all of their attention on joyful subjects. While I certainly believe in being positive, let me ask you something: Don't you consider it positive education when you teach your children to avoid high voltage power lines and when schools conduct fire safety drills? I have heard a parent say, "Well, I rely on the Lord to protect us." To that parent I would say, "Do you take that same approach when it comes to keeping small children from running into the street into the path of an oncoming car? Might not that be abdicating parental responsibility?" Don't play the ostrich and put your head in the sand. In my experience, it's not safe there!

Trust that still small voice that tells you something isn't right in order to avoid tragedy. If I had learned what I now know while my daughters were young teens, I believe I could have saved my daughter's life. Therefore, I have been on a mission now for quite a few years to try to save the life of your daughter, son, granddaughter, daughter-in-law or possibly your own life by sharing in my speaking and my writing some of the things I have learned.

First, you should know that 80 percent of violent crimes are committed by people known to their victim; and second, the vast majority of violent crimes are crimes of opportunity; so when it is within your power, don't provide the opportunity. To help you recognize signs of danger, I want to describe some actual events that were crimes of opportunity.

An elderly grandmother drove into her upscale neighborhood in Dallas one morning on her way home with a load of groceries. As she got out of her car with an armload of groceries, she fell and spilled the groceries. It so happened that a young man who was walking down the sidewalk saw what had happened. This "nice young man" came to her aid, helped her to her feet, insisted that she sit to recover on her front steps, and retrieved her groceries for her. Then he joined her and sat down beside her to chat. When she told him that she was all right and that she was going to take her groceries inside, he politely insisted that he would do it for her. She allowed this stranger to follow her around to the backyard of her home to the kitchen entrance. When the lady tried to take her bag from him at the back door, he ignored her and said, "We'll just put them on the counter before I go." Unfortunately, she followed him into her kitchen. Once inside, away from the view from the street and her neighbors, he brutally raped her.

This was a stranger crime, which statistically make up only about 20 percent of violent crimes. My daughter's case fell into the 80 percent bracket. The man who killed her was no stranger. In fact, there is evidence that the first three of the four women he murdered knew him. Serial killers usually evolve, killing someone they know before graduating to the murder of strangers.

Since I never had a chance to interview the lady who was raped, I wondered if there was any point before the actual rape where she experienced a sense of uneasiness or fear. If so, she must have dismissed it as "just being silly," probably believing that a man who behaved so courteously surely could not be capable of inflicting harm.

There are times in life when a fear response is appropriate. At such times, this sense of fear is actually a gift. This initial feeling is often a vague sense of uneasiness. I heard Gavin de Becker, an expert on threat assessment, say that we humans are the only creatures who will walk right into a situation when our instincts are telling us things are just not right! It is vital that we pay attention to this tiny impression. Don't be dumber than a wild animal. Leave the scene. Don't get into that soundproof elevator by yourself with a man who suddenly gives you a creepy feeling. Don't wait for confirmation until you see red lights flashing and alarms ringing. By that time, it is often too late. In the case of my daughter, both of us had disquieting feelings about the man she was seeing, and both of us rationalized them away. I had never been taught to trust that gift of fear, so I could not teach it to my daughter.

Con artists, sexual predators, and other felons often employ psychological tools to persuade you to do what they want you to do. The man who raped the elderly grandmother used five of the seven ploys that Gavin de Becker writes about in his bestseller, *The Gift of Fear*. (1) He used the ruse of charm. De Becker reminds us that charm is not a character trait; it is a way of acting. The young man had the grandmother thinking he was a nice, thoughtful young man. (2) He made her feel in his debt so that she would allow him to get her away from the view of the street and the neighbors. (3) He assumed a nonexistent bond between them, as if they were in this accident together. He used the word "we" as if they were now a team. (4) He brushed right past the word "no." When you say no, say it with authority. Don't enter a negotiation; just keep saying no. (5) He offered her a promise that he would leave once he had put the groceries inside. Never trust a promise from someone that you don't know. A sociopath will have no qualms about breaking his promise.

When my friend Myrtie told me this had happened to a friend of hers, we discussed it. Being a Southern lady and a gracious hostess, Myrtie admitted that if someone had helped her with her groceries, she would have felt obligated. In spite of knowing what misplaced trust had cost my daughter and this elderly friend of hers, she admitted that she would probably not have made the connection, and under similar circumstances her natural reaction would have been to offer him a glass of tea! When I heard those words, I just screamed in disbelief! It was scary to me, because I feared my friend would rather risk her life than appear rude!

And then there was Lisa. I know this teenager's story well because her stepmother is a good friend of mine. Lisa had come in from school and left her home briefly to call to her brother in a neighboring yard to come home. When she came around to the front, she saw a brown car parked in their driveway. At this point, there was at least a question in her mind about what the car was doing there, because she went on to state that she "assumed it belonged to friends of the family who also drove a brown car." She continued through the garage to the steps leading into the kitchen. There she saw a young man whom she did not know standing inside the doorway to the kitchen. He immediately spoke to her in a quiet courteous tone and asked her if her father was at home.

If there were any hints of unease in Lisa at this point, the stranger overcame them simply because he was nice. He used his charm to rape her with the intention of killing her and almost succeeded. She said later that she thought he was a workman who had come by to put some finishing touches on the family's new home. In this case, he used a sixth ploy by asking for her help. She supplied him with facts that he used against her. She told him her father was not at home. When she was asked when he would be home, she unwittingly gave him additional information that let him know he could commit rape and murder and have ample time to make his escape. He lured her inside the house with an innocent-sounding request. He asked for a pencil and paper to write down her father's phone number in order to call him. (She still thought he was a workman.)

Be wary when a stranger asks you for help. The convicted serial killer Ted Bundy confessed that he made it a practice of playing on the sympathy of young women by wearing a cast on one of his arms. He would ask for assistance in getting packages into his van. If a woman complied, she came close enough to his van for him to push her inside, and she then became his next victim. Child molesters often ask a child's assistance in finding a lost pet.

Remember: Trust that uneasy feeling!

Lethal Friendship...
a Mother's Battle to put and keep a killer behind bars
by Sue Young

For a glimpse into a vastly different kind of friendship, go behind the scenes with author Sue Young in her book *Lethal Friendship*. While experiencing the unfolding of this riveting, suspense-filled true story learn to recognize clues that could save the lives of those you love.

To order go to: www.lethalfriendship.com

About the Author

Sue Young's friendship with Mary Kay spanned 30 years, during which time Sue became Michigan's first Mary Kay sales director. Her first book, *Lethal Friendship* was about a very different kind of friendship. Sue holds a BA from the University of Texas and a master's from Duke University.

Printed in the United States
144330LV00005B/19/P